The Scars You Don't See
Moving Beyond the Challenges of a Dysfunctional Family

by
Dan Sherwood

With Natalie Windsor

READ THIS FIRST

If you come from a dysfunctional family, your story is unique and true. This book is to acknowledge you, validate you, and support you. It's not a contest to prove who had it worse. That would miss the point. This book is about your results, not your horror stories. Whatever flavor your family's "dysfunctional" was, you had to work with what you got there, and when you went out on your own you carried that imprint with you. Whether the warping happened directly to you or just around you, you received the pain—and the long-term effects.

Instead of viewing your childhood through a lens of self-blame, try considering yourself as a result. You grew up in a twisted environment. Because of what we received, witnessed, coped with, and internalized, we see adult life through a skewed perspective. What we attract probably wasn't as expected.

Be forewarned. This book is very naked. It exposes a lot of myself, with the intention to serve and support – it's much less painful to look at the childhood experiences of someone else, growing up with distress and confusion. The anecdotes included here illustrate the results of thinking warped by growing up with "normal" nowhere in sight, not an attempt to appall or outrage. This book wouldn't help anyone if read for shock value or defensive comparisons. You may see yourself in these pages, and understand what we learned and *didn't* learn. You can gain new insights, and realize how much more success and satisfaction is available for you.

This book is about your getting *better* results. Even if a dysfunctional family molded you, there's a way to a better life experience. You can create and experience more joy, and build healthier relationships, because it all starts with your relationship with yourself. If you struggled through a confusing, painful childhood, the real challenges began when you left home. Here we will confront our challenges and manifest new results.

CONTENTS

INTRODUCTION: WELCOME TO THE ER

Ever feel socially estranged, or "less normal" than other people? This book is for you. Got a friend, co-worker, or employee who doesn't feel completely "normal" to you? Here's a peak into the heads of people who learned to think and feel differently from you. We live in a world that pressures us to fit in, and meet other people's expectations. We're expected to be "normal." How's that been working for you? Many people live in a "psychosocial no-man's land," in "normal's" gray area. Whenever it seemed like you've been in situations where everybody else had some secret knowledge you didn't have, or understood situations that felt completely alien to you, you had good reason. What happened? Let me shed some light for you.

I work in an unusual helping profession, with the job title of Clinical Vocologist. Primarily, I rehabilitate and retrain professional voices, helping people who use their voices for a living recover their voice quality and vocal strength after injury or illness. Therapists like me help people who need to discover—or rediscover—their natural voices. My training in three additional alternative practices also improves breathing and relieves chronic aches and tensions. Faulty postures and breathing patterns contribute to voice problems, but they can also trigger psychological problems, even panic attacks. A problem with your voice, muscles or skeleton can literally change who you are, because how you sound and look to others are basic elements of your identity.

I'm one of many people who arrived in a helping profession not by accident. I come from a dysfunctional family. You're likely thinking, "Yeah, right! So does everybody else." Imperfect families are everywhere, but truly dysfunctional families are a different bucket. Try this on:

When I was 15, I was in my bedroom one evening listening to

my mom and 17-year-old sister fight at the other side of the house. I couldn't hear what the fight was about, but they went at it for quite a while. I don't know if my dad was even in the room. Mom eventually laid down some ultimatum, then things took an ugly turn.

"I hate you," was the next thing my sister spat. It's not uncommon for teenage girls to blurt that out when they're frustrated, and most parents know how to receive it. They let the kid cool off and get over it. That didn't happen in my house. As soon as those words left my sister's mouth, our dad leapt in, screaming in rage: "Get out of here! I hate your guts! Get in your goddamn room!" I cracked my door open just enough to see him kicking her as he shouted. She rolled and crawled, screaming in panic at being kicked down the hall. She had her own reaction to this treatment of daddy's little girl. I, watching it, wasn't as shocked or scared. This wasn't unusual. I was used to crazy shit like that. I was just glad it wasn't me this time. "Dysfunctional" involves and affects the entire family, no matter who did what to whom.

Childhood experiences like this develop "wounded healers"— grown-ups who enter helping professions, whose scars come from childhoods shaped by damaged adults. If you're from a dysfunctional family, this is your practical guide from someone who *gets* you. The obstacles created by your past gave you difficulties that are shared. I get you, because I've been you. If you'd appreciate a "straight from the horse's mouth" perspective, you got it.

The after-effects of a painful bizarre childhood can be tackled in more than "Anonymous" groups, counseling offices, or websites when you're alone in the dark. You can uncover your exceptional self once you can rewire your thinking and apply new ideas. You are meant to thrive and be exceptional, even if your childhood didn't set you up for it. Your relationships, with others and yourself, can all be understood and remedied. You can change your relationship to a past you had no control over, and create a better future.

Read this to learn why you are the way you are, and why things have happened to you in your life, and how you can change it. You'll understand what's driving choices you've made, and how to make choices that serve you better. For years, a lot of questions didn't seem to have answers: Why did I make so many social blunders? Why did I feel like I always wore out my welcome? Why did I let people treat me so disrespectfully? Why did I feel like a broken outsider?

Growing up with chronic stress, trauma or fear warps us and sends "normal" running for cover. The result is a skewed adult life. Are you one of those people, or do you know some? It's more prevalent than you realize. Many people feel stranded in the world. They don't all become violent criminals or wind up on the street. That's a stereotype of people from "broken homes," but the reality is that we blend into the community and can be productive citizens like many others. But we don't feel normal, and it's revealed in our personalities, in the ways we treat ourselves and how we deal with other people and let them treat *us*.

You've seen other books about adult children from dysfunctional families. Maybe you thought they related to you. Some of what they said might have been true or helpful, but how many of them were written from the outside perspective of psychologists, social workers or clergy? This book is based on real-life, first-person experience and insights. It's not a second-hand taste of someone else's experience followed by professional analysis. I'm willing to be candid, raw and honest, to serve you.

We carry the mindsets and habits of our families with us into adulthood. We don't get our education in the schools we attend

3

as much as we get it in our living rooms, kitchens and hallways at home as we grow up. We may not recognize the effects of our childhood experiences; or we might even deny them. After many bewildering, angry-at-the-world (and more often, at myself,) years, not comprehending what was going on in my head or my life, I started to see how the past was screwing with my adult experience. And I decided, "Enough already!" Is it time for you to do the same?

We don't need "recovery." No one is ill. Coming from a dysfunctional family is not a diagnosis. This is a book to lead you into discovery and blossoming. It will offer you easy, productive ways to modify, accept and even celebrate yourself. With patience, persistence and intention, learning to embrace being "different" and "unconventional" can be an advantage. With open-mindedness, some direction and a bit of effort, "dysfunctional" can be replaced by "exceptional." This is a do-able game plan to get you there. People who transcended painful pasts can help you transcend, too.

A challenging childhood doesn't have to follow you like a mongrel dog. Plenty of people can say, "I grew up in a crazy, dysfunctional home and I turned out fine." Good for them. That's one story. You are a unique individual, and you are not alone.

This book will serve you by sharing someone else's experience. It's easier to see the point when you don't feel it's aimed at you. You can read what it has been like to be me, but you may also see some of your own story and become aware of yourself in new ways. In many ways, this could be an autobiography-of-us-all. So many of us grew up in the pain and confusion of dysfunctional families, I could have many co-authors. This book was created to share specific ideas and positive practices, derived from spiritual and philosophical teachings, and mind-body disciplines. Even though what's on

4

these pages may not describe your experience exactly, it could strike a familiar chord.

Think of a hospital emergency room: everybody's wounds are different and were acquired individually, but they've taken everyone to the same place. There are no unaffected spectators in a dysfunctional family. Whether you know it or not, you're in the ER.

Here, we can unpack our conditioning and quit re-creating past painful, confusing struggles. Once you can recognize and understand your sensitivities, habits and tendencies, you can learn and practice alternatives – and see better results. Get unstuck from your inertia. Put in a change. This book will give you ways to grow beyond your early conditioning and start changing how you think, feel and behave. You can transform what has been an uncomfortable liability into an asset. This book can show you how much you've already begun.

1 THE INTERSECTION OF *NORMAL* AND *NOT*

Some people are different because they choose to be. Others are different because they can't help it.

Putting the word "me" next to "dysfunctional" is uncomfortable. It brings up thoughts of people who are weird, brash, socially awkward, who don't fit in. If that feels like part of your experience, read on. To start making positive changes, you have to first "meet yourself where you are" and be willing to take an honest-with-yourself look at just where that is, and how you got there. Some of us need help to recognize the effects of a painful, not-nurturing early environment. Some of those effects are obvious, and some not so much.

Everyone collects a few scars as they go through life. We get our cuts and scrapes, have accidents or sometimes have operations that leave visible scars as we heal. Those are the scars you can see and tell stories about. Our scars are the ones you can't see. Revealing and talking about them isn't easy; they affect us in ways the outer scars don't. We can change how those scars affect us. We can undo the conditioning that contributes to self-defeating thinking, and move beyond the thoughts and feelings, misinterpretations and reactions that developed when we were at our most vulnerable.

How would you define "dysfunctional?" I hope you didn't hear in your house what I heard in mine. *"I wish you was dead*!!*"* my mother screamed at my father during an intoxicated rage. *"You dirty stinking bastard!"* rang in everyone's ears as she stormed her way through the diatribe du jour. Dad's response was usually to sit there and take it until he'd finally had enough; then he'd leave the room. Sometimes, he would launch a verbal counteroffensive, and I'd hear a cruel shouting match between two people whose marriage had seen better days. No wonder mom had to take blood pressure medication, and dad popped antacids throughout the day. We kids paid a different price, one that lasted much longer than childhood.

Full frontal dysfunction is regularly being pulled into frightful, appalling episodes while you grow up. But a kid doesn't know that. You just have to hit what's pitched and live in whatever world your family creates—it's your regular everyday experience. Living in a climate of tension and anxiety, of dealing with persistent anger, fear or shame is your reality. As far as a kid knows, it's every family's private reality. It isn't. You'll feel the consequences of that reality as your life unfolds. What you learn about relationships, how to "love," and how to raise children is completely messed up, to put it mildly.

The emotional scars you collect growing up in stress and dismay complicate life later. Words in some families can be ugly and painful: "You are without a doubt the *dumbest* thing!" my father would yell whenever I had an accident or made a mistake. Imagine the lasting impressions left on a 10-year-old, held down and beaten in front of his friends for using the same foul language heard at home every day. Painful to witness, let alone endure, but my childhood friends saw my sister and I suffer that raw humiliation more than once.

The people who raised us had their own considerable issues. Here's part of the menu:
   o   Addiction or substance abuse (choose your poison)
   o   Unmanaged or "self-medicated" depression or anxiety
   o   Anger control issues
   o   Physical violence toward the spouse or child
   o   Narcissism, jealousy or rivalry between parent and child
   o   Self-indulgence to the point of child neglect

Regardless of the specific reason, the result is the same: you don't get the childhood you think other kids get, and the effects stay with you. Your parents may tell themselves they're nurturing and teaching you to like and believe in yourself. Is that what you got? When you're raised by people who are "under the influence," emotionally or chemically unglued, overwrought, mean, or who need adult supervision themselves, their problems are your problems. There's no place to hide.

Nobody had a perfect childhood. Every family has its problems and conflicts. It doesn't mean your life is ruined if you saw your parents fight, or if there was occasional drama. But inflicted turmoil, embarrassment, and a frequent sense of dread is like having a bad roommate who won't move out. Growing up, you feel a gap between what you *do* know and what you think you *should* know (what everyone else seems to know.)

How tense was your childhood? How brief? Dealing with unhinged adults can force children into artificial early maturity. When you're preoccupied, distressed or distracted by what's happening at home—or something you fear is happening— you're unable to be a regular kid, socially and emotionally. You can't navigate adolescence well to become a successful adult with the beliefs, attitudes, and coping strategies you developed at home. You're not sure what *normal* is, but you're sure you're not it. You're left to figure that out on your own, by trial and way-too-frequent error. How could you resolve this continuing struggle if you grew up in an environment full of *ab*normal? In this book, we're going to do it.

People with vocal injuries remind us that every problem has a source. A constantly rough, raspy, or weak and unreliable voice calls awkward attention to itself. People think you're getting sick and politely ask if you're feeling okay. A voice problem directs more attention to your sound than to the words you're saying. When we take on the behavior patterns of our families, people aren't always so polite if we're socially awkward. If you grow up hearing hateful, violent speech, getting pulled into scary, high-decibel brawls or mortifying public scenes, or if you're denigrated and disrespected by the people who raise you, you end up with issues of your own. Often there are problems with trust (trusting too much and too early, or never trusting anyone), lack of self-respect, defensiveness, honesty, and more.

Ask yourself some questions:
- Am I comfortable meeting new people, making good first impressions and keeping a conversation going?
- Do I feel socially competent? Are people sometimes put off when I don't keep quiet, or when I could have said something more tactfully?
- Have my relationships been successful, where I've felt like, acted like and been treated as an equal?
- Am I nervous and anxious around angry people? Do I blame myself when others are upset?
- Do I feel good enough for anybody—worthy of love and respect?
- Do I understand my feelings? Do I even know *how* to feel sometimes?
- How much do I beat myself up for my mistakes?
- Do I feel like a phony, like I'm just faking it?

Considering yourself dysfunctional sucks as much as denying it. If you feel stuck, or like you're just getting by, the joy and satisfaction you see other people enjoying is also available to you.

You can deconstruct your childhood experience. Crack it open and discover what growing up in a toxic, self-destructive home may have done to your life—likely completely under your radar. You can't "just get over it" without understanding what IT is, so you can make informed, life-improving choices. Let's devote our energy to turning around the effects of a childhood spent in a dysfunctional family. You deserve self-enrichment, creating and sharing more joy, developing your spirituality and attitude, your posture and language, even your diet. All these and more play a role in growing into who you want to be. You don't have to stay stuck in the mold of your childhood. You can identify it, understand it, say "Enough already!" and choose a new path.

You can discover and retrieve your missing pieces. Many of us leave home without knowing what's missing. Then the confusions and frustrations pile up. You fail where you see others don't; you feel isolated or badly different. It's not just you. I get it; I spent years there. I did dysfunctional, so *you* won't have to any more. If you don't like and respect yourself and draw the "wrong" people to you, if you never give yourself a break for your imperfections, then it's time for transformation.

I spent half my life envying others who I thought had what I didn't have (better life circumstances, relationships, possessions.) I took everything personally and let myself get hurt and angry. I automatically viewed situations from a victim's perspective. Any advice or perceived criticism felt like a personal character assault, and I'd defend myself ferociously (I suffered through my annual work performance reviews in self-defense, when they were supposed to be productive dialogues.) I didn't feel worthy to make eye contact with anyone. If that sounds familiar to you, know that you have the power to step away from your past burdens.

Your new life is just beginning, and you can accomplish amazing things if you're willing to recognize then repair the issues your "other than normal childhood" created. Why not? You didn't cause it. It wouldn't be your fault even if you wanted it to be. You were a kid stuck in a hostile environment, without any power. But you have the ball now. You don't need to re-live your childhood, or analyze it to death; you can understand it differently, even be grateful for it, for the special tools and strengths that it gave you. Moving beyond the residues of your upbringing starts with the way you think—your attention and intention. You can create a new template for your life by applying the ideas you read about here. You'll see how your experience can change and pull you towards a more rewarding future, instead of continuing to be pushed along by a past you neither created nor deserve.

Ready?

2 CALL IT WHAT IT IS

It's all right to say it: "I come from a dysfunctional family." See? The sky isn't falling. Just say it. You're not judging yourself or complaining about your parents, you're only stating what is. Besides, when you give something a name it can become familiar and less intimidating. The word "dysfunctional" carries an unpopular stigma. Sometimes it's a punchline in TV sitcoms. It's not used casually here. Most people can't understand it the way you and I do, especially if they didn't experience it. But what does it mean in real life? Introductory Psychology textbooks define people from dysfunctional families as individuals who have trouble behaving normally, especially socially, who have trust issues, and who struggle in relationships. That's fine if you're taking Psych 101 in college, but what if it's been your daily reality since you were a child? What if *you* are the textbook in your life experience?

Outside-looking-in perspectives have limits. What's really needed is a combined inside-looking-in-*and*-out approach, to understand who we are and where we come from. You're reading that approach now. Empathy, professionally-trained guidance and objectivity can take us far, but no one can walk a mile in our shoes. Nobody can go back to your childhood and re-live your developmental years. Talking should lead to taking action—from theory to practice. No action means getting stuck in a cycle that sounds like "recovery" but doesn't pay off. Our upbringing can't be erased. We can't undo, un-see or un-experience the effects of our early years—they're like our psycho-social fingerprints. But reconciling or making peace with the past is not the goal. The results are better keeping the focus on here and now, moving forward. However, don't ignore the influence of your early history and its impact. Your past has plenty to teach you.

Textbook definitions don't accomplish much beyond description, because your experiences are unique. Your feelings are about what's going on inside. We don't wear signs. Our scars are hidden. Most people from dysfunctional families are outwardly no different than anyone else. But **"dysfunctional" isn't just about what went on in your house; it's about what's still going on in your head**, which invisibly influences what goes on in your life. Our subconscious minds shape the way we see ourselves, how we frame and interpret our experiences, and how we use and sometimes abuse ourselves. The crap we internalized as kids shapes our facial expressions, our postures, the words we speak and the way we speak them. Our feelings and behaviors are basically the results of programming that was corrupted.

Knowing the name and source of a problem isn't the same as fixing it. Even if you know that your father's anger or your mother's drinking, for example, are reasons for your thoughts and feelings, it's still up to you now to make the corrections. Growing up in tension and discord is the reality you had to endure when you were too young to understand what you were facing. If you've been blaming or denying up til now, notice that it hasn't solved any problems. While it's not your fault if your personality or communication skills formed in ways that aren't serving you now, you can step up and make the changes you want. It's work, but it's worth it.

The cliché says we have to own behaviors and admissions in order to change them, but clichés become clichés by being so true so often. Frequently, we don't know what we don't know, and don't even know how to ask. Because it's easier to learn from others' painful experience, I'm going to confide some embarrassing moments of my own—minor ones, but very illustrative effects of growing up in "other than normal."

15

In my 20s, I would regularly attend professional meetings or accompany my general manager to upscale restaurant meetings with clients, while wearing a dress shirt and tie – and high-top basketball shoes. I probably should have known better, but I didn't. It never crossed my mind that I might have looked immature or less than professional. That style worked for David Letterman on TV back in the day, but I wasn't David Letterman, which is what my boss ultimately had to tell me. I was so embarrassed. I could tell he felt sorry for me, and in a fatherly sort of way he tried to educate me and, as he put it, to "bring me along" socially. As for dress shirts, here's a similar humbling example: When you get dressed and tuck in your shirt, you're supposed to also pull it out a bit to blouse it, right? I didn't learn that until I was almost 30 years old! And I had always wondered why everyone else looked so much nicer than I did in dress shirts. Thank goodness someone finally clued me in. Lots of little things get dropped in a dysfunctional home—the training gets lost in the family drama. Many basic social graces weren't developed while I was growing up; my young mind was too focused on coping with conflict, chaos and people's volatility. You can't practice a "normal" you didn't learn.

According to John Dewey, some of our early family and community associations can be "hostile to the realization of a full personality." Were the actions in your house hostile to your development? How often have you created the same dynamics with other people? Hostile relationships become expected, and it's well known that we're drawn to what's familiar. The circumstances you come from—and tend to re-create—become part of your identity, like your voice. What if you don't like your voice? You can't take out your larynx and put in a new one; you develop what you have. If you grow up in fearful, volatile situations, your body acclimates to the feelings and behaviors of dealing with stress and angst. "Normal" is just a blur. Your nervous system looks for its fix of distress and chaos. It's almost automatic to find or create adult relationships like your family dynamic—that's how your subconscious knows you're you. Names and faces change over time, but not much else does.

Even if you could recognize that your experience was abnormal when you were a kid trapped in a dysfunctional family, you had no power to change it – then. You were just a child trying to cope. You couldn't know how it would affect you in the future. You may feel somehow passed by, wondering "what the hell?" The ways you've learned to relate to people don't always work, and set you up for problems as you transition from teenager to adult. How were those years for you? Were you liked and respected by your peers? What kinds of people and experiences did you attract? As teenagers and young adults, my sister and I pulled into our lives a lot of people who took advantage of us or used us, and we were often rejected because our social behavior wasn't right. My dear sister had to go to three different high schools before she could graduate—not because of the academic demands, but due to social problems. She had made so many enemies that she needed to escape to other schools because of threats to kick her ass. Many girls made her life terrible, by passing hearsay and rumors about stolen boyfriends and inappropriate behavior.

If your personality and people skills developed in a climate of pain, mistrust, mixed messages, shame, or anger, how can you grow to be a person who others enjoy? Navigating a "normal" childhood and adolescence is challenging enough. What you learn during those years you bring into adulthood; it's your "baggage." Have you been confident and successful with potential romantic partners over the years? Or have you made up a reality that wasn't there and then paid for your assumption? It's a part of re-creating what might be the only relationship dynamic you know. I know I did it, and it often pushed away or contaminated what could have been good relationships. See if one my experiences sounds familiar:

I dated a doctor for a few months when I was in my late 30s, the result of a well-intentioned setup. We had tickets to a popular play one night and had the opportunity to attend a pre-show talk by the director. We made plans for a full evening: a nice dinner, get to the theater early for the director's presentation, and enjoy the play. Things didn't go the way we had planned. When I picked her up, she asked to make a quick stop at the mall, so she could pick up a new pair of glasses. She said it would "just take a second." It didn't. The place was crazy busy that evening, so we waited... and waited... and waited. It took forever. I knew that time for personal errands and a social life was a luxury for medical residents, so I was nice and understanding, and I wanted her approval. When we finally got out of the place we'd missed the chance to go to dinner and still get to the theatre on time. She suggested we save time by grabbing a quick snack in the food court and eating on the way. There we were, sitting in my car in the middle of the mall parking lot eating slices of food court pizza. Hindsight being 20/20, I should have had a sense of humor and just rolled with it, maybe joked about how glamorous a doctor's life can be. Ha ha.

No.

I was too stressed, nervously anticipating having to defend myself and calm her down, worried about how upset with me she would be if we were late. Repeated experiences with my mother, and later with other women, drove me into my reflex pattern; their frustrations were often taken out on me. To make matters worse, we ran into a traffic snarl on the way to the theater and missed the pre-show activity after all. As we crawled along the freeway, I was fidgeting in my seat and angrily shouting at the traffic. I replayed a familiar scene that was wholly unfair to her. In my mind, I totally wrote her dialogue for her, not giving her any credit for being flexible or good humored, even when she said, "It's fine, we'll get there." Do I need to tell you that the relationship didn't last much longer?

Do you know what loving, stable relationships look or feel like? Think about the relationships you've been in, or may be in now: mutually respectful and beneficial? Or more one-sided and unsatisfying? Part of the reason my marriage failed is that I didn't know how to be in it. I had no idea how to be someone's boyfriend or husband, and my spouse had little tolerance for that. She wanted an adoring, doting partner or there'd be hell to pay— I had attracted someone with issues left over from her own unusual childhood experience. My reflex was to go along to get along. But I eventually grew tired of being hanged for every real or perceived mistake I made, and when I started pushing back, the relationship deteriorated. Two people make a system. It's rarely one person's fault when a marriage fails. If one or both of you is living in fear of the other's wrath, ultimately, one or both will be resentful.

How do you handle disagreements? Can you be assertive and stick up for yourself? If you grew up with torment and hurt, you're probably going to do what you *learned* to do when attacked – do you shut up and take it, or have an outburst? Do confrontations make you tense and nervous? How do you typically respond in arguments? I've almost quit jobs because of ill will after ugly exchanges with co-workers, exchanges I never saw coming. Sometimes people get uppity in the workplace, they pull rank or push to put you in what they feel should be "your place." Rather than respond in a nasty firefight, I'd often swallow my pride, and get passive-aggressive instead. Old training dies hard, but you can find inner peace through simple spiritual practices, that you'll discover in the next chapter. You can change your approach to uncomfortable confrontations. You'll discover that in the real world—as opposed to the house where you grew up—you can assert yourself without all hell breaking loose on you, in you or from you. If you're calm and civil, there's no need to get aggressive or even passive-aggressive. You can let your past habits die.

19

No matter what your intentions, passive-aggressive behavior won't always let you sidestep potentially ugly confrontations. In your family growing up, direct confrontation was probably a painful mess, which may have conditioned you to avoid it. But if passive aggressive behavior was your childhood solution and it trailed you into adulthood, it's not just unproductive, it's unflattering and makes you look childish. An example from my young life: My high school Sociology class read *Lord of the Flies*. After reading it, we were put into groups with an assignment: What would you do if your group was stranded on a deserted island? My group gathered and discussed survival and rescue plans. I sat at my desk by myself and wrote my own plan: I would piece together a small shelter, away from the group, build campfires, fish and forage for my own food and water, and practice my martial arts on the beach. I didn't dislike the others; I just felt unwelcome. The next day, when each group's representative presented the various plans to the class, my group wasn't going to get full credit—my signature was missing from our plan. Because I hadn't even participated, the rest of my group began calling me names and angrily ridiculing me. My outburst was an angry challenge that surprised everyone, including me. "What are you assholes going to do, beat me up!?!" The teacher came over with the group's paper and I signed it without further ado. The guy sitting in front of me was our group spokesman. He turned around and said, "You didn't want to get beat up, huh?" I happened to be chewing a piece of bubble gum at the time (don't tell the teacher); I snarled and spit it across the aisle at him. Not exactly a healthy normal response. The next day, the girl who had been sitting next to me all year moved to another part of the room, commenting with contempt, "I'm not going to sit by *him* anymore!"

Adolescent habits don't go away by themselves. When I was in my early 30s, I had a high-profile afternoon-drive radio show at a station in the Midwest. Part of the job involved periodically doing remote broadcasts at advertisers' businesses. I did a remote one Saturday at a home electronics store, and I wore a plain shirt instead of something with our station call letters and logo on it. The sales person who had organized the broadcast was expecting me to show up in my "colors." She voiced her disappointment to our general manager, who told my program director, who called me into his office on Monday and told me the boss was unhappy with me. I didn't think it was a big deal, but it was their turf, so I apologized abjectly. I was hurt, and felt I'd disappointed and angered people whose approval I depended on, but I was also mad at *them*. I had delivered the highest ratings in the station's history for them, but that evidently wasn't as important as a polo shirt with four letters on the front. The episode should have ended there, but I reverted to passive-aggressive mode. I never said anything verbally, but I wore the station's branded clothing to work every day for the next two weeks—t-shirts, polo shirts, sweatshirts, baseball caps, jackets, every piece of promotional gear they had. The boss was no dummy, and before the end of the second week, I was called back in the program director's office and told to knock it off if I knew what was good for me.

If your family was like mine, confrontation manifested with shouting, threats or its own unique brand of crazy. Clashing in mature, healthy ways wasn't the norm, but bizarre thinking or weird outbursts were what was taught by example. When I was 14 years old, my complaints about my mom and stepdad's behavior were met with "You wanna say that in *court*?" Or I'd be told to "Go in the backyard and bang your head against the wall," if I complained about how much booze was being swilled in the house and the unholy mess it was causing. Kids in dysfunctional families live an uncomfortable contradiction: we had to grow up fast, but we may also have matured "behind schedule."

If you're not safe to assert yourself at home, or the way you observe adults carrying themselves is weird or downright scary, you're not left with good examples. Instead of learning productive behaviors, like when and how to self-advocate and assert yourself appropriately, you might react with open hostility and sound like you're looking for a fight. One of the marks of a dysfunctional family is that the adults in charge think and act in extremes. If that's the template you learned, you'll lose. You'll lose face, and you'll lose the respect of those around you. When it's time to be self-assertive, you might come off as coarse, belligerent or childish when that's not at all what you meant. Changing behaviors like that will demand consistent self-monitoring, but that becomes a habit that requires much less effort over time. I've learned that if a cashier gives me the wrong change, for instance, I can be mindful about how I point that out, so I won't look like an ass. Bad attitude is never my intention, but the habitual response was what I learned in my childhood home. Even simple, everyday exchanges can become tricky if you're not paying attention.

Consider trying to pause and choose your words, facial expression and tone of voice to fit your intended outcome—not to indulge yourself in the moment. This takes practice. You'll refine your ideas and choices all the time, and the choices you make can give you power. Psychiatrist Viktor Frankl developed a philosophy while he was imprisoned in a Nazi concentration camp during World War II. He eventually developed those thoughts into an effective therapy approach. Years later, he wrote, "Between stimulus and response is a space. In that space is our power to choose our response. In our response lies our growth and freedom." Write that on a sticky note and put it on your bathroom mirror. You'll benefit from reading it every day.

"Dysfunctional" is not a simple term—we all share certain hurts, and we all have uniquely different experiences. Fundamentally, it's about the things we were supposed to learn while growing up and didn't; and it's about things we *did* learn at home that don't work elsewhere. As we grew older, we often had the same thought: that once we left home to be on our own we could live the way we wanted to, and everything would be better. No more dealing with all that bullshit from home. That's true, but with a surprise. You got to be a grown-up, but without many of the necessary functional skills. There's no one to debrief or retrain us when we leave home. We go out and operate in a world we aren't necessarily prepared for. We've been socially and emotionally malnourished. So, it's okay to call your history what it was. You don't need to examine what's bad or good, just examine what *is*. Nor should you point to the past and blame or feel bitter. There's no insight or progress to be gained from blaming. This is about the process of overcoming the effects of a past you didn't deserve and thriving despite those circumstances. You're here doing it right now.

3 FIND YOUR MISSING PEACE

When we come into the world, we can't know what our family experience is going to be, what we'll have to face during childhood. We might get dragged into our parents' marital problems, or we could take on the role of caretaker or confidant for badly behaving adults. Maybe you had a parent who was jealous or felt somehow threatened by you because you stole attention from them, or they made you feel mediocre or like a burden. In my house, I might as well have had a referee's uniform and carried a whistle, I was so often dealing with people at each other's throats. But other times I had a target drawn on me, catching a verbal attack or a surprise backhand for an offense I didn't even know I'd committed. I learned the painful way to be careful when I opened my mouth.

One evening when I was twelve, I was upset because I couldn't find something I wanted to bring to school the next morning. My dad heard me whining about it, got up from the television, and quickly found what I wanted. He angrily shoved it into my hands. I said, "I didn't see it, so don't get all huffed up." Suddenly, he broke the Native American-style wooden peace pipe I'd made in Cub Scouts on my head: "I'll get huffed up if I *want* to get huffed up!!" I had to put an ice pack on the knot. I hope you don't have similar stories.

Anyone can have a bad moment and "lose it," even in a healthy family. But what matters is what happens the most. **Childhood experiences, good and bad, get processed in a child's mind, and the conclusions can stick around for a lifetime**—conclusions about self-worth, relationships, how to deal with stress or conflict, everything. We don't just "grow out of it;" as we grow, we can find ourselves stuck in self-defeating patterns without knowing why. Changing the venue doesn't change our programming. We don't simply go off to college or get a job and move into an apartment and not have our childhood experiences affect us. You need to change the programming.

In my mid-20s, I shared an apartment for a few years. We had people over one night, and I brought out a CD I wanted to play for everyone. My roommate didn't want to listen to it. He put up his hand to stop me and declared, "Please, I don't feel like doing that right now." This flustered and angered me. I felt rebuked and bullied in front of our mutual friends. Rather than stick up for myself and ask our friends if they wanted to hear it, I spent the evening quietly stewing, embarrassed and pissed off. Later, in the middle of the night, I picked up some books and threw them against my bedroom door in a rage. A moment later my roommate asked from the other side of the door if I was okay. I mumbled something incoherent, and he went back to bed no doubt wondering what was up with me. He had no idea what happened. He'd just asserted himself, and all I knew to do was to feel affronted, shut down and act out. I didn't know whether the others would have wanted to hear the CD even though he didn't. Would it have killed him to just be nice about it and suck it up for a few minutes?

We think we've "survived" our dysfunctional upbringing, but if everything we learned there comes with us unchanged, we may have made it out alive, but we brought it with us. Picture a rescue dog—beaten up in a former life and slow to get close to people, fearing or detesting, or practically giving yourself away to anyone who shows you approval or affection. You're not a rescue dog, of course, it's just an analogy. Even though your childhood is over, the emotional byproducts are still within you. Survivors merely live to tell the tale, and you deserve better than that. Once you identify the patterns (which we've begun describing) and start changing the habits and behaviors that followed you out of your home, you can go on to thriving. So, how do you do all that with an unstable foundation?

26

First, be aware that you're more than you think. Thriving begins with finding peace – peace within yourself. Sounds nice, but where does that come from? *Peace* and *dysfunctional families* don't fit together. How do you get "spiritual" if that's not part of your background? If it is part of your background, how does it benefit you? Is spiritual development worth the effort? It is, if you want to get yourself to a better life experience. Even if you're leery of spirituality and agree with Jean Paul Sartre's philosophy that we're just "thrown into the world," someone or something had to do the throwing. You are connected to that "thrower." Your childhood experience may have set you off-course, but you can get back on course, using your connection to your Source. If you believe in a Higher Power or Higher Consciousness and have faith, you can seek a deeper or different understanding of that relationship. If you are ambivalent or don't give much thought to the idea of a God or a Higher Self—or are an outright atheist not on speaking terms with a Creator—if no one is listening, what do you lose if you explore it anyway?

Some young people's lives have no time for spiritual *anything*, they're so inundated with family drama. Some young people's lives are so overwhelming that they do the opposite, and retreat into desperation or prayer. In some families that are hyperreligious, the children are browbeaten (and sometimes physically beaten) into submission by overly stern parents who can't provide a happy childhood. Your spiritual awareness will be a process, possibly a very gradual one. If you're patient and willing to receive teachings from objective people and reflect on their ideas, you can find your missing peace—a peace you might not have understood in the past. It can happen, and it will begin enlightening you from the inside out. Others got there, so can you.

At the time of my divorce, I was in a town where I knew hardly anyone. My ex took custody of most the friends, so I was alone. The few people I did know encouraged me to stay busy and get out of the house as often as I could. "Go to the bookstore and read in the coffee shop," a co-worker recommended. "Just get out among people," she said. I could do that. There was an independent bookshop in town attached to a nice coffeehouse. I began reading philosophy books first, then I moved onto chaos theory, mind-body practices, and eventually spiritual literature. Looking back, the progression was natural, since spiritual traditions inform many other fields. Every inspiring idea I tried to understand and bring into me made me a better human being—less angry, less defensive, less abrasive, more approachable, more peaceful. Now I share them to benefit you. If you keep an open mind, you could come to the same valuable realizations.

For a moment, consider your true origin: a Higher Consciousness, even before your painful, dysfunctional family. Before the people who raised you were thrust upon you, something else was going on. You were—and always have been—part of a field of Divine Intelligent Energy. This isn't proselytizing or selling abstract philosophies, this is just an encouragement to accept yourself as something more than your human experience, to discover your Higher Self. Joe Dispenza reminds us, in *Breaking the Habit of Being Yourself*, "You are energy with a consciousness." This realization will let you start creating amazing experiences in your life.

Believing that you are part of Divine Creative Intelligence can be a life-altering revelation if you're willing to work with it. This is more than a simple realization or a private affirmation, it's a relationship—your connection with that Intelligence. Relationships take effort, nurturing and intention. If the notion of spiritual development makes you uncomfortable or resistant, don't think, "Oh geez, now he's going to start preaching to me." Don't worry. That's not what's happening.

Developing a relationship with your Source (or whatever name you give it) manifests necessary, positive results. It's a Source that many of the most hardcore scientific minds have accepted, acknowledging that there's an Intelligent Energy at work. Instead of imagining a Guy with a beard on a throne, consider an Energy that connects everyone and everything. Accepting a Source doesn't mean subscribing to a specific religion or going to church. You may or may not be doing that already. You can connect with your Source, and benefit from it, whether you identify with or follow any organized practice. You'll find that spirituality and inner peace are like transmission fluid in your car—a little may be all you need.

Religious and *spiritual* are not the same. Both empower you with new ways of thinking and of finding peace. Both can help you see yourself and others as equally worthy of peace, joy, and the best of life. Jane Roberts, writing as "Seth," wrote in the early 1970s that "A soul is not something you have. It is what you are." But spirituality doesn't have to mean worshipping a Supreme Being. It's about creating a partnership. Some people are more comfortable using terms like Source, Divine Intelligence, or Higher Consciousness. Those are all synonyms. You can discover new directions and set up more pleasing interactions with people when you're aware of being part of a greater whole. No matter what traumas you endured growing up, you can practice new ideas to bring you to a new emotional and spiritual place. Try these on one at a time. See how they fit for you, and see what starts changing in your daily life.

Whether you realize it or not, you already have a support system: The God (or Source or Creative Intelligence, etc.) within you, your connection to the Creator. Any spiritual development gives you strength, possibly even a sleeping strength that's been waiting to come out. Cultivating peace inside you creates peace outside you. That inner peace helps you avoid situations where things you mis-learned growing up might surface and cause you to say or do things that make you look bad and feel worse. Or make you look bad when you don't even realize it.

"But I'm doing fine." Of course you are. Old emotional scars don't manifest 24/7. If they did, there would be no hope. But there is hope, and growth, and success. Each dysfunctional family is damaging in its own way, and our lives have their own unique experiences. We also have a lot in common. You can recall times when you've felt embarrassed, humiliated or angry because you didn't know what to say or do, or when something you said or did put other people off when you didn't mean to. Maybe you took something personally that others would just blow off. You might be calling up your own list of examples. I'll share a couple of mine as relevant illustrations.

When I was 20, I went to the movies with some friends one evening. The theatre became very crowded as people filed in. A couple made their way through my aisle and sat down. The man got up for a trip to the concession stand. A minute later his wife got up and asked if I wouldn't mind saving their seats for them. I kindly obliged. When she returned, I joked with her about being displaced in my seat for them. She knew I was kidding, and we smiled at each other. When her husband returned armed with popcorn and worked his way through to his seat, I glanced over at the woman and gave her the same look as before. We again exchanged smiles. A few minutes later, they decided to move to some seats nearer the front. As they walked by, I curled up in my seat and made another sarcastic comment to the woman. She smiled at me knowing I meant nothing by it. Her husband, however, glared down at me, and with a threatening tone said, "Look guy, if we want to walk by, we'll walk by; you got a problem?" (I remember it word for bloody word, like it happened yesterday, even though it occurred in the 1980s.) I said I was only joking with them, and they went on.

Of course, my friends and the people around us saw the exchange. I felt like I looked like a wimp, but it's hard to do well in a fight when you don't know you're in one. I fretted over it as the movie started, feeling humiliated and stupid for not spouting some clever comeback and looking like a wuss in front of everyone. I worked myself into a quiet little fury. Within ten minutes I was so mad that I politely excused myself, abandoned my friends, and I walked over five miles home. It never occurred to me that the attitude problem might have been his. The habits I learned from my upbringing made the responsibility and shame all mine.

As adults, we can learn hard lessons in social awareness, if our childhoods were mostly about crisis management and insecurity. When I worked in radio, my co-workers sometimes admonished me for saying inappropriate things to station advertisers. I often had no idea when I was inappropriate or offensive—I was just being me. Even though I enjoyed good ratings for my work on the air, with my coworkers I was often considered the eccentric, and not taken seriously as a professional. At that time, knowing what wasn't socially appropriate was not my strength. The trainings of my childhood would often cost me—in my job, and in my relationships. One year, the sales manager at a station where I briefly worked generously invited me to his home for Thanksgiving dinner. I sat at the table with him, his wife and his in-laws. As dishes were passed around, I made a comment about one of them that I thought was funny. I was mistaken. My colleague dropped his head as his family sat there in uncomfortable silence. Later, he took me aside and reminded me that my show wasn't back on the air until Monday and could I please stifle the off-color remarks for now. I was so embarrassed, I wanted to crawl in a hole and die. I didn't leave, like the movie theater; but at work, I steered clear of him for weeks afterwards.

31

Since we didn't learn what "normal" is, we don't always make good first impressions or know how to change the ways we're perceived. We internalize our anger and frustrations, because we've learned bad consequences come from reacting out loud. Before I learned new ways to operate, I would get mad and avoid anyone who called me "out of line"—whether I was or not. Thinking, "Arrogant fuckers!" was the only way I knew how to think, back then. Growing up, I didn't learn enough about what's always appropriate, or how to repair a situation after a mistake. Or how to tell constructive criticism from snarky self-indulgence, or how to accept and use the good stuff. If you feel like you're seeing any of yourself in these examples, you can do something about it.

Without good examples growing up, we need to acquire better role models; otherwise, we avoid confrontational or embarrassing situations and often mismanage what we can't avoid. Acquiring simple spiritual practices eliminates the need to make defensive smart-ass comments or trying to sound witty. You won't embarrass yourself trying to win people's approval. You won't automatically jump into negativity, aggravation or self-criticism over inconveniences or moments of defeat. Everybody makes mistakes. We all put a foot in our mouths sometimes, but we don't have to automatically beat ourselves up for it. **Learn to let go of the ego's needs. Ego is the barrier to success.**

We have better things to do than let ego govern our lives. Ego wants approval. Ego can't stand losing face, and it bruises easily. Growing up in a dysfunctional family teaches the ego to take out its frustrations on You—experience teaches us that directing frustration or dissatisfaction outward usually results in disaster. How many times did your protests about something you didn't like end up right back in your face? Mentally replaying defeating experiences teaches you to punish yourself for mistakes, even mistakes someone else made, that you take responsibility for. The choice is simple: learn to live "in Spirit" or be stuck "in ego." With just a small shift in awareness and some practice, you'll find that being governed by Spirit rather than ego is a much more pleasant way to live. You can get to Spirit and notice a significant difference: peace within you.

One of my duties in the voice clinic is to perform laryngeal stroboscopic exams—the medical term for "sticking a camera up through the nose or into the mouth to the top of the throat so we can see the vocal cords." (Don't worry, we numb the patients first). If someone's breath or mucus blurs the vision, we can clear the view with a few drops of defogger on the lens. That usually nets us clear pictures of their vocal cords moving and vibrating. Developing your connection with Source is the defogger for your spiritual lens, when ego mucks it up, distorting how you see yourself and how you think others see *you*. Ego denies, accuses, and negates spirituality. When you can practice living in a way that is more Spirit driven, you roll with life's punches more easily. You're set up to thrive, to prosper – the way you're meant to.

Thinking, habits and attitudes you developed as a child can be restructured and upgraded. Easy spiritual practices are a good place to start, calming your body and mind and guiding you to a place where there's no angst, no impatience, no starving for others' approval, no seeing things from a victim's perspective. Let's tackle the spirituality-based ideas and practices first, then move to other life-enhancing ideas.

Promoting spirituality is not so different from internet dating. (Stay with me here). In online profiles, you'll see people refer to themselves as "spiritual but not religious." With one click, we can put ourselves into a vague category that looks good on paper but doesn't really mean anything. Think of spirituality like your voice. 'Voice' is both a noun and a verb. As a noun, voice is a sound—with pitch, volume and a quality, like clear, breathy or raspy. But you *use* your voice, it's more of a verb. You *voice* something—sound comes out of you because of intention and muscle activity. Spirituality is also more like a verb than a noun. It's a concept, the understanding that life has a connecting Intelligent Source. But to be effective, spirituality is also something that you *do*, a way to live your life with a sense of appreciation and deeper meaning. As a verb, it's how you align with your Source and let it guide your attitudes and behaviors.

You have a range of options for spiritual practice. You don't have to dive headlong into anything, you can just experiment a little and find what you're comfortable with. Yoga, Transcendental Meditation or Asian martial arts and their spiritual aspects are wonderful. Zen practices or other Eastern-based traditions are also effective. Jews, Christians and Muslims can pray, read Scriptures and be mindful of their conduct according to the teachings of their faiths, even if they don't choose to affiliate with organized religion. There are many entry points into spiritual awareness, but it all begins with realizing that you are connected to that Divine Source or Divine Intelligence, if you make the choice to do it. Call it anything that works for you. There are plenty of choices: God, Creator, Higher Power or Higher Self, the Light, the Tao, the Universal Matrix, Brahman, whatever. What you call it doesn't matter. What does matter is knowing that your life is more than the result of human biology. You are a manifestation of Source, and your Source is patiently waiting to help you create.

You don't need to become some spiritual ninja or try to change the world. The real goal is to adjust your own inner world. This makes your relationship with the outer world more positive and fulfilling. One of my Somatics teachers expressed this idea by sharing a classic quote: "The meaning of life is to discover your gift. And the purpose of life is to give it away." Your gift, to discover and share, is what you can become, and create, when you connect to your Divine Source Energy—the

34

God within you. Before you leave your house every morning, take a moment to reflect on the Energy that created you, surrounds you and supports you. Notice how different that feels, from the common "another day another dollar" outlook.

Recognition and gratitude are two ways to connect with your Source. Please indulge me for a personal example. One Saturday at Whole Foods, the man in front of me in the checkout line had gotten lunch from the food bar. He was paying with a gift card, but the cash register wouldn't take the card. He didn't have any cash on him, and the cashier had to summon the manager, who unsuccessfully tried to help him, creating delays and fuss. Thankfully, they treated him respectfully. From the looks (and smell) of him, he may have been a homeless person who might have fished a used gift card out of the trash. I watched the whole thing, and offered to help. He graciously let me buy his lunch and he thanked me, saying, "That's very kind." I said, "My pleasure. God bless you." He gave me such a smile. This story is only minimally about me. I was glad to be in the right place at the right time *for him*.

Every day, look for opportunities to express your connection to Source. You'll feel kind, but you'll also be connected to your Source and to your fellow human beings without the intrusion of ego. Most of us have had moments where we've lent a hand to a stranger. Didn't it feel good? That's a *source-filter interaction*. Simply explained in voice therapist terms, the vocal cords (source) make the vibrations, but the sound needs the throat (filter) to make the vibrations strong and meaningful—just the intention doesn't produce useful action. This is an important concept in vocal therapy that applies directly to how we can live. You can be the throat, so to speak.

The source needs the filter to magnify it. The filter needs the source, to have something worth magnifying. For your voice, that's resonance, a transfer of energy (more in chapter 12).

Apply this concept to your daily life. Your source is *the* Source, the Divine Intelligent Energy that created you. You can filter that Source Energy through you. If you want your life to be better, adopting a Spiritual practice and putting the intentions into small actions can magnify and enhance your Source Energy with wonderful results. Intend to live each day as who you really want to be. Start wherever you are. It doesn't have to be *every day for the rest of your life*, just *Right Now*. You're on the path to thriving, starting with your peace within, your connection to what created you.

Growing up in distress, confusion and uncertainty can be a crucible for developing addiction. Addiction to what? Basically, approval. We can want it so badly that we give up a lot of ourselves to get approval from the adults who have control when we have none. We've been trained to turn over our happiness to other people, and we can feel like we're not allowed to be happy unless someone we've given the authority to is happy *with* us. The pattern functions almost stereotypically like an addiction: get a taste of approval and need how that feels, and we come back again and again for more. But the dysfunctional controller doesn't always dispense what we're hoping for. We keep coming back and trying, because any little bit of approval meets our needs and feels good, temporarily giving that artificial high – things will be okay for a while. We keep coming back, sometimes satisfied, but more often let down. The pattern is set. That's addiction. You deserve better.

That could be a reason why some people can't seem to stand being alone. If they're dissatisfied with their own company, and need the constant approval of others, they can criticize and feel superior without ever being self-critical. Some of us might be the opposite and isolate ourselves, possibly battle-fatigued after years of working to keep the most important people in our lives pleased enough not to explode on us or freeze us out. Does that inspire, "Welcome to my world" under your breath? You're not alone. If you learned this in an environment that didn't make sense, where the rules randomly changed every day, now you can learn to give up your addiction and take back your power to be happy.

The changing moods and mixed messages of a dysfunctional family can literally make you crazy. If you heard "You're my angel" or "What would I do without you" as a child, did those words hold up? Kind, supportive, nurturing words spoken in calmer parenting moments are crazy-making when paired with cruel and confusing outbursts. When it served them, we were approved of and the folks at home were happy with us. Parental approval is more than gold to a little kid. But if you're approved of one moment but treated like shit the next moment, that's going to trash your self-esteem, if you can hold onto any at all. You are addicted. That won't set you up for social success as a teenager or an adult—just the opposite. Approval addiction is a frequent characteristic in adult children from dysfunctional families. Professional literature usually stops at basic descriptions. So, let me give you some real-life translations.

I had one girlfriend for about two weeks during my entire adolescence, and I didn't lose my virginity until I was many years older than my peers. Most men wouldn't admit that in a million years! But claiming my history is part of my overcoming and thriving process. I didn't know how to be in a healthy relationship, or be happy in one. My family experience essentially caused me to grow up fearing women. I wanted attention and approval from the opposite sex, but I didn't know how to get it in any "normal" way. If I did get attention and approval, it was only a matter of time before the mismatch of styles and values ended it. I felt tossed aside, slandered and not good enough. My early environment set me up to find women who were unkind, rejecting or with abusive personalities. As a young man, I was just out in the world without a clue, feeling I was making a fool of myself or putting myself beneath other people to deserve their approval. Most of my relationships as a teenager and a young adult, both personal and work-related, weren't based on mutual respect or equality. I'm willing to share my experience, if it serves you by example.

One of my first jobs after high school was as a delivery driver for a printing company. It was a low-paying, entry-level job, not meant for educated people with marketable skills. My fellow drivers were all about the same age, 18-21, but we had little in

39

common. They liked to party. Drinking and recreational drug use were their pastimes, not mine. But I wanted their approval and wanted to fit in, so I lowered my head and propped them up by giving them my approval. At that time, the best way I knew to get along with people was to let them think they were cooler and more popular than me. That was the approach I developed in high school. I even wrote an essay about it for one of my senior English class assignments: "Better Than Me." My teacher, Mr. Koenig, was so concerned—I think I blew his mind—that he told me I "might want to talk to the counselor" about what I had written. I ignored his advice and just kept going the only way I knew how. When I finished high school and entered the workforce, I was accepted and liked, but I was treated the way I set myself up to be treated—as less than, as an oddball. If you're nodding your head because you've had similar experiences and feelings, it's time to stop looking for approval in all the wrong places.

You set yourself up for disappointment or even heartache when your happiness depends on someone else's approval. A translation of Verse 9 of the *Tao Te Ching* reads, "Care about people's approval, and you will be their prisoner." Say it out loud. This is a profound teaching. Your happiness can't be based on what's happening outside your control. Your happiness is a natural result of your connection to Source—what's within you. Happiness was given to you by your Creator. Your job is to say thank you and enjoy what you were given. Imagine God Himself saying, "I gave you the power to create. Get off your butt and start creating!" You'll discover how much more is inside you than your childhood conditioning tells you.

A dysfunctional upbringing replaces self-generated joy with self-doubt and confusion. It helps to have guides or examples who demonstrate what joy is like; and we can't pre-judge where we'll find those guides. Some teachers you can seek out deliberately through workshops, books and training programs.

Others will emerge at unexpected times and surprising places – once you start. This can be a challenge when you're younger and still living under your parents' roof. When I was a teenager and began studying martial arts, my saluting a new authority made my dad jealous and resentful at times, seeing another adult male having such a strong influence on me. It was common for him to lash out when he felt usurped. But there was one instance when a valuable teacher showed up unexpectedly.

When I was 16, I ran into a bee while riding my motorcycle home from school one day. It slammed into my arm at 35 mph and stung like hell. I got home and put an ice pack on it, but the ice didn't help much. My forearm swelled to about twice normal size, but I tried to tough it out. That evening, my friend Mike and I went to my karate instructor's house, to watch an old film we all wanted to see. Sensei looked at my painful, red, swollen arm and was concerned that it might be an allergic reaction. He suggested I have a doctor look it over to make sure everything was okay. When I got home, I asked my dad if he would come with me to the hospital ER, since I was a minor and on his health insurance policy. He blew his top, ranting and yelling at me in front of my friend Mike. "Why don't you have him put some of those goddamn 'herbs' on it?!?" he yelled – "him" being my sensei. With no shortage of fury, we drove to the emergency room. As we waited to see a doctor, I apologized to Mike for dragging him along and keeping him out later than we had planned. "It's okay, don't worry about it," he said. "I care about *you*." Hearing Mike say that seemed to calm my dad's anger—at least making him consider that he may have overreacted—and that his kid's welfare was more important than another scotch and soda. My buddy Mike was an important teacher, one of the most selfless and kind human beings I had met in my young life. Tragically, he was hit by a car and killed when he was 27, but I still learn from him, even today.

If you're open and observant, you'll find many teachers. Whom do you look up to? Would you think of Forrest Gump as a role model? Usually, watching a movie, we expect to be entertained for a couple of hours without looking for deep meaning. But some movies can be unexpected surprises. *Forrest Gump* was a touching Oscar-winner with some meaningful lessons. Here was a simple guy, perhaps a kind of savant, who lived an extraordinary life by merely surrendering to it. Forrest Gump had no agenda. He didn't know how NOT to be loving, non-judgmental and God-governed. An ego has an agenda and wants approval. Forrest got approval by simply being who he was, without getting hamstrung by people's opinions. He was a fictional but well-written, genuine character – a good teacher who demonstrated how to live a Source-connected life, without relying on others to make him happy.

Let's go back to Internet dating. We know it's not 100% successful (duh). Lots of us go on those websites or use dating apps to look for love, hoping to meet someone who will make us happy. That goal requires another person, which means we have to exert the effort and time and hope to find that person. (Remember, each of us is a God-particle, already wired for fulfillment and joy; we just need to assert ourselves as such.) You won't find happiness just by getting together with another person who is also looking for you to make THEM happy. That result is two people each looking for somebody else to create each other's happiness. If you can accept yourself and own your right to be happy, instead of mourning what you don't have yet, then you'll project a much more attractive energy to the world. You may find that "trying to meet someone to make you happy" won't be necessary. You'll attract who and what is right for you – the way you're supposed to. You will be a channel for the happy energy you'll attract.

Forrest Gump is a perfect example of the saying, "It's not the destination, it's the journey." Your journey can be a wonderful adventure, regardless of whatever hardships you endured while growing up, or since then. Remember, you are a Divinely-created Being, and that deserves value. In fact, you're saying a sort of thank you, each time you express your connection to your Source. Express that connection as often as you can. You might have to learn—or re-learn—how to make that connection to Source, but that's part of the reward of the journey. We get ideas and make discoveries as we listen, observe and learn. You'll discover yourself influenced and inspired, sometimes in unexpected ways.

If you're not sure where or how to discover your own Source-connected happiness, you can start by noticing it in other people. With your eyes and your mind open, you can find models worth following, and replace the ones you had as a child. Forrest Gump's character isn't corny, he's probably a much more optimistic example than your childhood role models. When you begin paying attention *with* intention, you'll start to notice and appreciate admirable qualities in other people; the exceptional ones will stand out and can become your guiding examples.

You might have a friend, a neighbor, a co-worker, or an acquaintance who has a special charisma or magnetism, they're that full of positive energy. Someone who easily gives and receives kindness and love, and their energy makes you feel good. Notice that they're not trying to *do* anything; they lead by example because that's just who they are. In his book *A Parenthesis in Eternity*, Joel Goldsmith writes, "There are many inspired and illumined men and women on earth who are totally unaware of that identity or of the individual source of their inspiration and strength."

You probably know at least one person who's that radiant— always smiling, vibrant, or charmingly quirky. The love coming out of them seems to fill the room. They're giving you more than their radiance, they're giving you their example. Follow their lead, it could be the direction you need. Think of the people you encounter every day. You may know some Gumps. You need them in your life. People who radiate a heart of gold, who perform even tedious tasks without complaints, who evidence little or no temper (Note: a 'bad temper' comes from ego). You know, the people you look forward to seeing because you feel better being around them. Why not be that person? Deliberately analyze their personal style. Be a little more like them, and add your own unique spin. Notice the enriching, fascinating people who can help you replace your childhood patterns. You only have to pay attention, with intention.

Be aware: the after-effects of a childhood in a dysfunctional family act like a computer virus. The "bug" invades you and quietly influences nearly every way you operate. Unfortunately, there's no tech support to remove the virus for you – you have to do it. And you can. (More about "virus removal" later in chapter 11.) Our early experiences and conditioning affect our decision making, our emotions, and how we evaluate and respond—in every interaction. Before every word or thought, the climate you grew up in enters and shapes it. Do you always see and interpret people and circumstances accurately? Everything gets filtered through a warped lens, "Just as a man with green spectacles he cannot take off is sure to see everything green," wrote Bertrand Russell.

Since your past experiences determine how you interpret every new experience, learning to see through new eyes and interpret things through a different mind takes intention and practice. Connecting with Spirit-governed individuals is one way to find that perspective. Once you begin changing how you see yourself and take on some new behaviors, the people in your life start to treat you differently, and your world literally changes. (This can come with some challenges, see chapter 13.) Creating stronger, more enriching relationships and more supportive circumstances comes out of self-love. Dysfunctional family? If we do the work, it's not just behind us, it's completely away from us.

We shouldn't need to *learn* to like ourselves, but the only "should" is in our heads. It's likely you develop an "I'm second-best, or less" mentality in a family that treats you that way. If you've absorbed that, and treat yourself as less worthy than other people, get real! That's not you! When you're willing to let your guard down and share a little of yourself, unexpected impromptu "support groups" can pop up. Don't be afraid. There are scores of people who will relate to you and validate you, if you let them. Trust them to let you be who you are.

Some years ago, I was in central Italy at a summer retreat for vocal performers. I went there wanting to learn more about singers' processes, to better understand their experience, to help more effectively when singers had voice problems. We spent the beautiful warm days working on group and individual songs, developing vocal technique and performance skills, and enjoying the overall fellowship. One morning, assigned to learn to give of ourselves to better connect with an audience, we were given an exercise to silently act out our life history in front of the group. This was daunting, but I took my cues from the others and gave it a try. When it was my turn to be an amateur mime, I got up and moved about the room, physically acting out my life story to that point. I would periodically yank myself backwards as if I had a yoke around my neck that wouldn't let me make any forward progress without a fight. This represented the past and the "I'm not good enough" mentality I was working to change. I must have been a pretty good mime; my fellow vocalists really nailed the meaning. A couple of them were almost in tears. This exercise wasn't supposed to become group therapy, but that's what happened. Others had life histories like mine, and it was a powerful, restorative experience getting that validation and support from each other. Some of us talked for hours afterward.

With time and patience, and following the examples of inspiring people you meet, you'll start to appreciate something that's possibly new to you: you have the support of your Creator and an abundant Universe that wants you to succeed and to love yourself. If this notion provokes some skepticism, that's okay. The idea of spiritual connection can seem a little airy fairy if it hasn't been part of your experience. But once you're willing to explore, doors can open that you didn't know existed.

You can create meaningful change by gradually chipping away at any resistance and considering new ideas. No need to go shopping for prayer robes or start chanting psalms; just realize you're not randomly adrift in the cosmos and that you can access other ways of thinking and being. Effort isn't necessary, only allowing. Sometimes, the more we *want* or *try* (for approval, affection, or sympathy, for instance,) the more frustration or disappointment we feel. "Expectations are resentments under construction," journalist Mark Schiff quoted. We get so goal oriented in Western culture, always wanting to achieve something. Sometimes it's better to just calm down and allow.

Let yourself be more like the ocean instead of like a river. A river moves, sometimes violently, and can destroy what's in its way. A river is like the ego, insisting. The ocean, however, allows. In discussing the *Bhagavad Gita*, Swami Satchidananda wrote, "The ocean is contented. It never sends invitations to the rivers. It's just happy to be itself. And that's why all the rivers want to flow into it." So be like the ocean – happy to be uniquely you. You are enough, a perfect product of your Source.

"Run, Forrest, Run?" Absolutely. You don't run away from the past. You move *towards* the life you desire and can create, beginning today. Listening to or reading the works of spiritual teachers, or people who teach how your thoughts become your reality is a great way to start shifting your attitude. Well-chosen support groups can be beneficial. Even taking advantage of

46

formal, insurance-covered therapy is not what it used to be. There are fascinating holistic therapies involving mind-body unity that are now mainstream. If you've tried and benefitted from any of these, keep going. Sustained positive practices and thought patterns create healthful change, just like seeing good results from consistent workouts at the gym. You'll become even more inspired as you experience the positive outcomes; new possibilities will emerge. You're creating momentum.

By adopting some of the ideas, or personal qualities, of spiritually-connected people, you'll realize what an admirable life you've already created, and can continue creating, despite your past conditioning. You're ready to reclaim your personal power and become the person you know you are, and offer that person up to a newly-appreciated world. This is your on-ramp to being exceptional, by practicing and allowing instead of wanting and trying.

Forrest Gump didn't want people's approval. He just allowed. If you remember the movie, you know that he was often made fun of and insulted; but he continued to quietly set the example, allowing life to happen and just being who he was, without being driven by ego. Eventually he had everyone's approval. We all have that same light inside of us, and by accepting it, we can attract amazing people and life experiences to us, and discard past conditioning. We can recondition.

Deepak Chopra reminds us that, "Through conditioning, we generate the same impulses of energy and information, the same behavioral practices that result in the same space/time events, the same biochemistry, and, ultimately, the same life experiences." Channeling some Forrest Gump—being positive, unprejudiced, kindhearted, and patient—is a way to re-condition. Create joy, within you and around you. You don't need to "light your candle at every man's torch," but you can pay attention and follow the examples of stimulating people and find a new balance. Keep your thoughts and behaviors in balance with what you want to bring into your life. In the next chapter, you'll see a useful way to find balance in your thinking and daily actions.

Fully discovering and repairing the effects of being raised in "other than normal" can get complicated. It's easier to change what we can clearly see and understand. The difficulty comes from us not seeing and interpreting things the way others do. We may be so used to blaming ourselves (or for some, always blaming others) if we're dissatisfied, or for whatever we feel our failings are, that we don't consider how our childhood training has jaded our perspective. But cheer up. If you want something better than what you've had, you can create it. Start now, by choosing how you're going to feel – what you're going to intend and project. Replacing what no longer suits you is a natural process. We see nature do it every fall.

Notice how encouraging everything looks on the first day of fall. Flowers blooming, foliage at its greenest before beginning the process of change. It's the equinox—equally light and dark, and nature in balance. Mother Nature is preparing to reboot, and what's coming could be beautiful. What happens naturally in the fall is a reminder of how potentially changeable *we* are, with the freedom to refresh our lives. Give yourself credit for the parts of your life that are in balance and satisfying. You did that. You can do more of it. What about the aspects of your life that feel out of balance? Do you look forward to the day, feeling good about where you are and what you're doing? Or do you feel stuck, or bored? Not sure how to get to what and who you feel you really are or want to be? No easy answers here. Self-analysis and reflection can take hard work, but the results are worth it.

Your childhood conditioning won't let go of you, *you* have to do the letting go. Being defensive, carrying a victim mentality or endlessly swallowing your pride for others' approval are attitudes and choices made from a badly warped perspective, consequences of the past. You can change that with a reboot of your own—a paradigm shift, in today's vernacular. It's very do-able. When you appreciate and exercise your power to choose, you start leaving behind the effects of an unfair, not-so-nurturing childhood.

The choice? Your feelings, which then guide your words and actions. You can feel happy, angry, sad, or hopeful, enthusiastic, whatever you choose. The expression that having an education can never be taken away from you is also true of your choice to feel and respond to circumstances in the way that supports the person you choose to be. That freedom can't be taken from you. Only you can give it up; or you can use it to your advantage. Every day is a clean palette with which to create something extraordinary, because you get to feel how you want to. Poet Carl Sandburg wrote of the fall season, asking, "Is there something finished? And some new beginning on the way?" Yep! You can begin anew every day and choose to feel good, positive, encouraged. Your state of mind is your choice, not something that can be forced upon you. Anticipate your day based on who you want to be TODAY, rather than giving in to the momentum of a discouraging past, even if you had a bad day yesterday and that's "the past."

As adults from dysfunctional families, we don't live in the past, but we often live *from* the past without realizing it. Your early learning and experiences inform how you process and respond to things now. (My personal examples in this book may help you realize your own habits and choices, and offer you different choices.) Obviously, the healthier and more enriching your childhood was, the less distorted your interpretations of others' words and actions will be.

Update the programming in your biocomputer—your subconscious mind—by setting an intention for the day, every day, and choosing to feel good. There's no such thing as "being in a bad mood," only making a certain choice. Disagree? "I feel how I feel." You're right. How you feel is under your ownership. In the movie of your life, you're the casting director and the lead actor. You choose how you want to feel, then... "Action!"

Change can feel awkward and uncomfortable, because you have to learn to recognize then alter what up til now have been unconscious processes. It's much easier for us *not* to change ourselves. But if you if haven't been leading the life that you'd like to (the one you know you're capable of but just can't quite get to,) then it might be time to shake things up. In chapter 12, you'll see how our posture and body alignment can affect our attitudes, feelings and overall presence, but to briefly fast forward: our uprightness and the alignment of our head, neck and spine is maintained by our habits. Over time, the way we carry ourselves, for good or ill, feels "natural" to us. Changing it—not sitting in the classic American slouch posture, for example—feels unnatural. The reality is that the posture and movement patterns many fall into are often the opposite of what's natural for the body. This is just as true of thought and feeling habits.

Every day is a fresh opportunity, so deliberately choosing to feel confident, eager and lively is a valuable strategy to start the day with. Set yourself up for a superb day by directing your thoughts to follow your feelings. Yes, sometimes this can be challenging, and in the next chapter you'll see one specific way to keep yourself on track. Our thoughts and feelings seem so reflexive and automatic. They pour through our heads so fast, tens of thousands of them per day. Trying to control every thought would be worse than herding cats. However, you can herd those cats to some degree, by controlling what you think *about*.

As you go through the day, a distracting "ball of yarn" may get dangled in front of you and challenge your intention. That is, thoughts will come up that don't harmonize with what you initially intended. That's fine. Deal with the incompatible thoughts when you need to, just make it a goal to match the intention you set at the start of the day, which hopefully is something like, "I choose to feel good, and everything I do today is going to support that." Cats operate mostly on instinct, but you have more than that—the freedom and ability to consciously choose. You can be different than those who raised you by not being impulsive or self-indulgent.

Treat each morning like the first day of fall. Everything is at its peak, ready to be harvested. It's like the equinox, perfect balance, a time to shed yesterday to make room for something fresh – and exceptional. Sit on the edge of the bed before you get up, and do two things for yourself: First, be thankful for another day of opportunity and possibility. A lot of people say, "Thank you" out loud at these moments. Say it. Then think about how you'd like to fashion the day ahead. Your intention is more powerful than you may know. Align your thoughts and the theme of your feelings with what you want. It may not be easy every time. Shit happens. Sometimes you get sidetracked. You'll meet occasional aggravations, or maybe run into nasty people who get in your face. But losing your cool and letting that stuff get the better of you just sets you up for more of it.

Everyone has probably been in a restaurant and had their order screwed up. If the staff isn't nice as you try to get things corrected, it's annoying. In the old "take my family conditioning with me" days, I'd often be abrupt and ill-mannered and make the situation unpleasant for everyone; then I'd stew on it and feel irritated long afterward. Life is too short for that crap. Here's a better choice: Intend positive feelings, and outcomes, during deliberate preparation of the day. Potentially negative situations can be diffused before they happen. You can do this.

If you want to feel good, and you want the people around you to feel good with you, your thoughts and actions need to support your intention. If you've nurtured positive, enriching thoughts earlier, you can radiate that energy. People appreciate it. Now, when I walk into a place for a coffee or to get the car serviced, for example, I make sure that my opening interaction with the staff is cheerful, energetic and good humored. I give 'em a little showbiz! It gets their attention in a good way, and lets them know that we're going to have a nice experience together, and that I'm a friendly person. If any mishap occurs, we're going to laugh about it. They'll take good care of me because I made the effort to establish good rapport from the beginning. Everything works out fine because that's my intention. This approach can work in just about any situation.

If there's only positive energy coming out of you, it puts people at ease and they'll feel comfortable. You'll get positive energy back from them. It's a little dance you do together, and most of the time it's fun. Granted, sometimes it can feel like a chore, but it's worth doing, because you deserve to have a good day. Start picking some situations and experiment with it. See what kind of results you get. You've done it before. You have a sense of humor. Share it. Give 'em some show biz!

Give yourself a break when you're not perfect. No one blames a tree for how it grew and the shape it took. It just responded to its environment. So did you growing up. However, big difference between you and a tree—conscious choice, the ability to visualize, use your imagination and think creatively. When you start imagining and visualizing what you want to have and achieve, it starts becoming yours – to do, to have, to experience, or to be! "Your successful performance starts in your imagination," many voice teachers have told me over the years as I've developed as a clinician working with vocalists. It takes thoughtful involvement and personal commitment, but that's how meaningful change happens; it's what practice is for.

Start every day on your own terms. Get your thoughts and feelings in balance with your desires. The results may happily surprise you, when you deliberately enjoy the feeling of already having exactly what you want. You're not playing a mind game, you're connecting with your Source, and creating. You don't get what you want by pushing it away in your mind, thinking that you don't deserve something or that it could never happen to you, or that "This stuff is bullshit." That's self-sabotage. You're more likely to get what you want when you first mentally and emotionally line up with it. Clearly create it in your mind, then live like it's already yours. You can "receive" it before you get it. Greet every new day like the first day of fall, the equinox, in perfect balance. Think about what you want, feel like you have it now, and radiate that energy as you move into your day. Herd your cats and enjoy the harvest.

6 KEEP GOD IN YOUR POCKET

To change our experience, we need to tackle daily life from a different angle. That means correcting beliefs that were laid onto you. Starting the day intending to feel good—or with meditation or prayer if you're inclined—will create a positive framework. The ancient Chinese philosopher Lao Tzu teaches this will help you adjust comfortably to the energy of the day. Anyone can benefit from a daily calming practice connecting you to your Source, but if you grew up where stress and strain were your "normal," it's essential for your growth and change. (More about this is coming in chapter 8.) In case you can't make the time, formal meditation is only one way to set up a successful day. Take one minute—literally, 60 seconds—to breathe mindfully. Pick an uplifting word to whisper to yourself, to prime your day: "peace," "strength," "compassion," whatever you want to receive and share. A simple activity that promotes a peaceful start to your day prepares you to thrive.

Set yourself up with serenity. Then get busy. You know you'll be pulled in a dozen directions as your day gets going. It's easy to forget your intention, when work and school and family demand your time, thinking and energy. You can mean well when you leave your house, but staying focused on who you want to be and how you want to feel is the challenge. If you saw the movie *The Secret* years ago, you may remember the guy who kept a small rock in his pocket. He would touch it through the day to remind himself to recognize and feel grateful for all the good things in his life. The results of that simple practice surprised him—gratitude is such powerful energy. You can follow this example.

Each morning, write yourself a small statement—an affirmation—that begins with "I Am..." Put it in your pocket, take it out and re-read it several times a day. Maybe you know, that I AM is one of the names God uses to us. In the book of

Exodus, when Moses asked what to tell the people when they asked who sent him, the reply came back "I Am That I Am. 'I Am has sent me to you.' That very 'I AM' is part of you and me; it's energy you can channel to support your intention. In *The "I Am" Discourses*, St. Germain reminds us, "When you say 'I AM' it is the full God-power acting, and knows no failure." Try it, you may find that 'I Am' energizes you.

When you deliberately start a sentence with 'I Am,' consider that you are declaring your connection to Source. It can be empowering. No one expects you to turn into some on-fire Bible thumper, or convert anybody. Call it a Supreme Being, just an Intelligence, or your Higher Self, but you have the ability to create. That's an asset that's always there to draw from, it's in you, not separate from you. Keep your little note in your pocket with the sentence on it, and look at it several times a day. It's a perfect memory prod to keep you on your intention despite distractions. Create your own 'I Am' statement, or one of mine may work for you.

I Am better than I was yesterday.
I Am becoming free of doubt and worry.
I Am attracting good into my life.
I Am surrounded by love, whether I see it or not.
I Am comfortable with myself.
I Am capable and creative.
I Am filled with positive energy.
I Am unlimited in my potential.
I Am in harmony with what I desire.
I Am focused on joy.

If you can't think of a sentence, a single word will do. Say it out loud and write it down: Composure, Resilience, Resolve, Empathy, Patience, whatever you want to give and receive today. Don't bother with flowery scholarly language, like it came from some lofty spiritual guru. It just needs to start with 'I Am' and state what you intend. When you need it, pull out the day's affirmation and re-center yourself. You'll discover how effective this simple action can be. For me, my little blurb in my pocket has helped me to think before I speak and to keep my mouth shut when I don't have something courteous and productive to offer. My co-workers no longer scold me for blurting out inappropriate wisecracks. Argentine writer Jorge Luis Borges offers good advice: "Don't speak unless you can improve the silence." Carrying your 'I Am' statement can surprise with wonderful results. Swami Satchidananda, in *The Living Gita*, reminds us of the value of staying connected to our Source throughout the day:

"Always keep your aim high to control the restless mind. If you meditate for 10 minutes a day but then just leave the mind uncontrolled to go where it wants the rest of the day, it's like holding the rudder for only 10 minutes and then leaving the boat uncontrolled, letting the wind toss the boat any way it wants."

Keeping 'I Am' in your pocket can be your spiritual rudder. It's easy, private and you can craft each sentence the way you want to, based on how you feel, and want to keep feeling. If you'd like a little more support, add other sources to keep you focused. Let me offer you a tool that's worked for me.

I used to drive past a theological seminary, but I always thought of it as "the monastery." It was a massive, charming old-world building—it could have been a piece of 18th century Europe, and the place gave off a special energy. It felt good to drive by it, imagining being part of such a close-knit spiritual community—meditating, studying, consciously connecting with Source. It was calming to imagine what it would be like to be part of such a fellowship, and live a more contemplative life, more in harmony with my Creator, not concerned about others' approval or disappointed with what my life was not. I could spend every day living "in Spirit." But you don't have to be a monk to allow divine energy to permeate you and reflect off you.

Try taking your daily moment.

One morning while driving by "the monastery," I wanted to somehow harness its spiritual energy and use it. Sometimes inspiration just strikes. "Just bring it with you," I blurted to myself. Simple enough—and so needed at the time. I was in a place where many of us have been, in need of a big life change so I could feel better about being me. I had to do *something*. I was hypersensitive and always wore my heart on my sleeve, practically brandishing a "Kick me" sign. When I made a mistake, got questioned or felt criticized, I would get angry and defensive, or mope in self-pity for days. If you've been there, you know that's no way to live. Here's the spiritual boost that was given to me.

Picture who you'd be, if you were as spiritually connected as you imagine the residents of "the monastery" to be. Would other people see someone kind, soft spoken, who lived simply and non-materialistically? Nothing is stopping you from becoming that person—especially if your life needs a change of direction.

That's easy to think about and looks good on paper, but the action of *doing* it is what makes it valuable. Part of my answer was to simplify my life, and to make even small progress each day toward my ideal. For starters, that meant downsizing and getting rid of things I didn't need or use. Donate it. You'll be surprised at how much "stuff" you can easily do without. I put a supportive phrase on my desk: "More Calm, Less Stuff." That was how I presumed the monks lived in "the monastery," Spirit-driven rather than accumulating material things or ego-driven. When I entered a helping profession, I tended to talk more than listen. Changing that made me a better helper and a better listener. That made me more accessible – to my patients, my colleagues, my neighbors, the cashiers at the grocery store, everybody. You can only benefit by simplifying, listening better, and becoming more Spirit guided.

60

The main premise of Rabbi Martin Buber's book *I and Thou*, is about the importance of relationships. Treating everyone as meaningful, acknowledging that everyone plays a role and remembering that we're all in this together is the attitude that will serve you—and everyone you deal with—well. Practice respectful, equal relationships with everyone, no matter whether they're long term or for the moment. Treat everyone with appreciation for who they are and what they do—friends, relatives, neighbors, your landlord, Uber drivers you may never see again. That's how I envisioned my attitudes and relationships would be if I were to bring the monastery with me. Audition this attitude if your current path isn't satisfying you.

Maybe your childhood hopes and dreams got pushed aside as you worked to survive your family's everyday antipathy. You may not have been allowed to discover your potential. Now that you bring "the monastery" with you, you can call on Divine Energy to help you become who you want to be, starting right now! It's the private mental practice that gives you some backup to make the most of the "I Am" statement in your pocket.

Early in my radio career, a dear friend and mentor taught me that "The secret to the universe is *access*—getting your stuff seen and heard by the people in charge of getting things done." At the time, it was about getting my vision and zany promotional ideas in front of the people who could help me pull off radio station contests and publicity stunts. It's still true. Now, it's about accessing Higher Consciousness—not getting others' attention and approval, or satisfying my ego.

How to get that access if you haven't been a spiritual person until now? Keep a daily "I Am" statement in your pocket, and imagine following the examples of the people in "the monastery." Just write it down: "I Am..." and finish the declaration with whatever you aspire to be. Do this every day, and remember you're not alone in wanting the best for yourself.

"I Am" gives you powerful access—connecting you with power bigger than just you, and making your intentions clear to the One in charge of getting things done.

We all need to take "me time" occasionally. Some call it "selfing," others say they're taking "down time." Whatever you call them, you deserve your private moments. You deserve to decompress a little and maybe get over a challenging day, to help you recuperate and stay grounded, or peaceful, or help you prepare for the day ahead. Taking "me time" is essentially a type of meditation. You don't necessarily need to sit in silence or repeat a mantra to be mindful and intentional with your time, and benefit from it. Take a little time to visualize—focus your energy on what you want, and how you want to create your life, and what you would do within that life. In the previous chapter, an "I Am" affirmation became your mind's rudder. Now the goal is to steer toward what you want.

Don't be seduced by the Internet. It's most often a distraction that occupies your mind in the wrong way – unless you're reading uplifting messages, listening to soothing music or motivating talks by inspiring people, you're wasting your "me time." Your "me time" comes with a proviso: Mean it! It's only for you. Following random people—or even friends—on Twitter, or casually meandering around the Internet is unproductive diversion. It can be the most peaceful, productive time of your day, when you clear your mind, reconnect with your intentions, and visualize yourself as exactly who and where you want to be. Some people say early morning, before sunrise, can be the best time of day for these moments, but you can find opportunities for "me time" whenever your schedule permits. There are many ways to get the most out of your "me time." Here's one way to do it.

You've probably heard of a vision board. Before making fun *of* it, have some fun *with* it by making and using your own. (If you do this in private, nobody will even know unless you tell them.) Focus your thoughts on what you want, and put that on the board. Close your eyes and visualize yourself living that life you've envisioned, using photos and positive phrases clipped from magazines and other places. What's the point of clipping out pictures and sticking them on a cardboard to stare at? For one thing, these are pictures of things that already exist, not dreams you've conjured up. In other words, **everything you want already exists**. It's already out there, waiting to welcome you. Put it together and make the visual real, so it's not just a fuzzy idea or a vague wish. What you want becomes concrete when you can see it. Then, you can claim it.

Focusing on what you want is not fantasizing, it's creating. Everything you want and can create starts with a thought, an idea. Think of it first, then visualize having or doing what you've created. Mentally experience the effects, the joys they bring—to you and to others. Doing that consistently, and committing to practicing it often, that thought-energy can inspire you to act, and access abilities and creativity you may have never realized you had.

Scientific research has shown how thought and intentions affect our reality. In the book, *Conscious Acts of Creation*, researchers cite controlled experiments conducted in two different university labs, that revealed effects of human intention on physical results. The experimenters learned and concluded from evidence that "humans can influence their environment via specific, sustained intentions." Visualize yourself where you want to be and with what you want to have in your life. Starting to move in that direction with your thoughts and feelings will influence your actions, and your actions will determine your results. You can bring in what you want by living the life you want, by being it starting now.

Feel a little cynical? So did I, at first. I made a vision board with the help and advice of a respected friend, and one of the things I pasted on it was a picture of a music room. While skimming through a pop culture magazine, I saw a picture of a room in a rock star's house, with instruments all around and comfortable furniture. That room was where the artist practiced and composed songs. It looked like a cool place, so I put it on my vision board. I'd visualize myself in that room, jamming on the instruments and working with creative people, regularly rehearsing that scene in my mind. Within two years I was working in that room—not an exact copy, but a room you'd never expect to find in a medical clinic. I was hired as a therapist at a prestigious voice center that was expanding to serve more performing artists. Part of that expansion was building a music studio, where we'd do vocal rehab with singers and musicians. I even got to help design it! Now I go to work every day in the coolest office in town. If making a vision board is not quite your style, that's fine. It's just one option. But look at the picture below and see what it's possible to create. That's my office!

Regularly pausing to focus inward is one of the healthiest things you can do. You don't have to use a vision board if you don't feel that it fits you, but you *can* visualize and see yourself in that visualization. Try this: sit in a comfortable chair, close your eyes, breathe calmly, and mentally create whatever life you want to live. See yourself there. How will you feel? What kind of person will you be in that reality? Likely, that's the person you've been waiting to be. So, stop waiting. You can be that person now! Do this, even once a day, and see what happens. What eventually shows up shouldn't be a complete surprise, because you intended it. Bring it to you. Start now.

Hockey Hall of Famer Wayne Gretzky said, "A good hockey player plays where the puck is. A great hockey player plays where the puck is going to be." So be a great hockey player. Put your thoughts where your life is going to be. Your results may not be an exact replica of what you've visualized, but the Universe has a way of conspiring to bring you precisely what you need. A mere coincidence when it shows up? Maybe. But you got it, and your intentions brought it.

If you've thought about meditation or visualizing as being too New-Agey, or if you've been resistant to spiritual practice, that's okay. Being a Western-acculturated guy, I used to think things like meditation and spirituality weren't masculine. But world-class athletes—both men and women—visualize themselves succeeding before their events, and there's no reason you and I can't visualize and intend our successes. Visualization as a daily activity makes it a lot easier to stay focused on your goals. Remember, you have an element of your Creator inside you. The Whole is embedded within the parts, and all of us "parts" are creations and reflections of that Divine Whole. Persistence does pay off. When you can allow yourself to be available to your own Higher Consciousness and start connecting to the God within you, you're linked to the Energy that will help you create the life you want to live, and to be the kind of person you want to be. Put your thoughts farther away from a negative emotionally (and spiritually) stagnating past. Play some great hockey. And get ready to ride your "me time" to a higher level.

Growing up in a painful, toxic environment distorts your thinking. It distorts the way you gauge and interpret others' words and actions, and how you manage relationships. You may not have even learned *how* to form healthy relationships; that not knowing can be confusing and frustrating. But if you've read this far and have been paying attention to "herding your cats," "keeping God in your pocket" and "playing some great hockey," you're already learning to live more "in Spirit." The benefits come quickly—expanding and improving your relationships, with yourself and with the people who are in your life, now and in the future.

Having a daily spiritual practice may help you become a better communicator, especially in emotional situations where things can often get uncomfortable. Heightened emotions can make it easy to retreat into old habits that don't serve you. But when finding some inner calm from regularly taking a few moments of quiet "me time," your responses in a delicate situation with someone are more likely to be positive and productive, rather than lapsing into old reflexes and behaviors. It's possible to avoid unnecessary misery. Here's an example of setbacks and miseries that could have been prevented.

At one point in my radio career, there was a day I was tasked with setting up everything needed for an early Friday morning special remote broadcast. That meant bringing and setting up and checking the equipment, props and everything the studio had that the location didn't. I needed to finish Thursday's work, in order to get home to bed, to be up by 4:30am. When I went to the studio to record a commercial before Friday, I discovered my supervisor using the equipment I needed. I must have shown my disappointment with having to wait inappropriately. He exploded in a rage—violently hurling a recording cartridge into the wall, disabling an expensive machine, and swearing at the top of his lungs. He'd apparently had a bad day and decided to take it out on me. Even if my reaction was a little selfish, his reaction was completely disproportional. I was no stranger to angry outbursts, but by then I'd been away from it for a while, so it took me by surprise and re-ignited old circuits in my brain. Can you guess my reaction?

I freaked out internally, and put the blame, shame and responsibility on myself. I was so upset, in the moment, all the way home, and all night. I felt I'd gone too far and it was all my fault. I decided my needs didn't matter. With only my childhood training to inform me, I decided that making my needs least important would be the solution to "my problem." My inner dialogue started with, "Who the hell do you think you are? You don't deserve favors for your convenience. Selfish bastard!" From that time on, I adopted the attitude of whatever self-neglect was necessary to serve the job. I thought that life would be a lot easier if I didn't matter. All that mattered was my shutting up, doing what I was told, getting things done, and remembering that I was not as important as anyone else.

I spent the next day in a dazed funk. When I saw him, my program director offered a lame apology. All day, I was too upset to eat, and even worried I might be fired for how I'd pissed him off. That evening, I sat down and typed myself a set of guidelines to follow. I taped it on the back of my bedroom door, so I'd see it every day: My sleep is irrelevant. My hunger is irrelevant. My comfort, satisfaction and convenience are irrelevant. My health is irrelevant. My happiness is irrelevant, and on and on. Now I know, these couldn't be more wrong! These are the lasting effects of a child's dysfunctional upbringing.

Remember George Orwell's *Animal Farm*? Think of me like the workhorse character Boxer, who kept saying "I will work harder," no matter how bad things got! I felt my needs and concerns were trivial and irrelevant, especially when I wanted everyone's approval. I thought they'd hate me if I spoke up. So, for months and months, I went far above and beyond the call of duty. Hours of my unpaid overtime didn't matter; working seven days a week didn't matter. Getting the job done was more important than ME. I'd remind myself that I was less important and press on, completely on autopilot, getting through each day the best I could.

That one triggering episode pushed me back into a role I knew too well: not changing, not growing, not understanding why I felt and acted the way I did. Five years later I recounted the events in a support group; everyone was angry for me. Because this reaction is common, they understood the feelings I was sharing and had similar stories of their own. They knew it was wrong of me to judge myself so harshly. They also understood the mindset that led me to do it. At the time, it was the only way I knew to handle it. I used to go on the air every day as a radio personality. I'd fake high-energy self-esteem very well. But when the microphone was off, I was a mess, hoping everyone would just leave me alone. The people I worked with didn't notice my sudden, exaggerated work ethic—or maybe they did, but it served their purposes. In fairness, I didn't notice their not noticing until years later, with the help of educated hindsight. We were all in our own worlds at the time. Eventually, I landed a new gig in a larger market and got out of there.

The patterns developed in a damaging childhood can reappear and surprise you. There's no statute of limitations in your subconscious. Overcoming the effects of the past takes more than merely escaping a dysfunctional environment. The first noticeable benefit of taking your contemplative "me time" is that it helps keep the fight-flight-freeze branch of your nervous system from making you emotionally fragile. (See chapter 16.) If formal meditation isn't for you, no worries. Periodically take a brief pause and pay attention to slow, relaxed breathing. This is commonly taught to voice therapy patients, because voice disorders are often accompanied by unhealthy breathing patterns, or paired with muscle tensions throughout the body. Paying attention to your breathing provides an instant mind-body link and can help settle down a distressed body *and* a distressed mind. (P.S. It's free!)

Take a seat, ideally in a recliner or a chair with an ottoman, so you're completely supported and not using your muscles to hold yourself up. Exhale, then take a gradual breath through your nose. Feel the lower half of your trunk (front, back and sides) change shape as you inhale. Make it a comfortable breath, not a big tank-up. Avoid high, tight breaths into your upper chest—that would activate the part of the nervous system you're trying to tone down. Exhale slowly, taking at least double the time you spent inhaling. This promotes a calming response in your body. Allow a natural pause at the end of your exhale—don't hold your breath, just wait. When it's time to inhale again, you don't need to "take a breath," just let go of the waiting. Let your breathing happen by itself, while you pay attention to its movement through your body. Breathe mindfully like this for just two minutes, and you'll feel at least a little better. This simple process helps activate the part of your nervous system in charge of rest-digest-heal, just like formal meditation does. Any time you pause and pay attention to your breathing, it can have the same effect as meditating, which promotes health. (Centuries of Yogi wisdom can't be wrong.) Some people combine meditation with affirmations—this can be twice as powerful if you're comfortable doing it deliberately.

You deserve brief self-aware time-outs, and they will make a big difference in your life. We all have our "If I only knew then what I know now" moments. When I look back on that explosive incident with my old radio supervisor, I know that the same episode couldn't happen today. My inner peace would give me the patience to not fuss over twenty minutes out of my life.

Today, I wouldn't help create the situation in the first place, and he could keep his bad day to himself. Give yourself some "me time," even if a few minutes is all you can find, to breathe and reconnect to your Source. Don't think of it as a religious practice—"religious" and "spiritual" are not the same, and "practice" sounds like work. Your Source transcends organized religion. Take time to re-affirm that you're part of Divine Intelligence; it's easier to stay centered and present yourself positively. You deserve to feel that good, and to receive from the people you care about what you're giving them.

The nice thing about meditating is that you can't fail or do it wrong. You just sit down, shut up and breathe. There's no agenda, nothing you're "supposed to feel." You don't need to download an app. Just BE. A mindfulness teacher once said, "If you want to be a cyclist, you have to get on the bike. If you want to be a swimmer, you have to get in the pool. If you want to benefit from Source Energy, you need to get in your own personal space, be quiet and listen to God." Allow yourself some silence for a while, and feel grateful for your "me time." Investing your time and intention will yield a return on your investment.

When you align your thoughts and actions with feeling good, you can expect that's what will come back to you. As others value you more, you'll see more value in all your relationships. As people can feel more at ease around you, they'll share more of themselves with you. (Hey, no one's comfortable sharing feelings with someone they think is a total spaz.) You'll also find it easier to share your own feelings—even bad ones—once you begin to take your regular "me time" and let yourself unwind. You'll start processing your emotions from a healthier place that you create, rather than from old toxic patterns. Everybody who grew up in chaos, confusion and dysfunction needs this kind of "me time." More of my story may feel familiar.

As a young adult, I became extremely uncomfortable when anyone around me got upset and emotional—in my family, that never ended well. I would try to stop people from getting angry or frustrated, even if they had a good reason. In my mind, they would aim their anger at me, until they'd finally burn themselves out. They were the tornado, I was the trailer park that got flattened while they moved along with no thought about the havoc they wreaked. So, I couldn't handle anyone expressing anger in my vicinity. That didn't help me make or keep a lot of friends or potential girlfriends or a spouse.

Sometimes people get aggravated and want to vent, even if it doesn't really calm them down much. Psychological studies conclude that aggravated venting doesn't really calm people down much. In fact, they tell us that venting anger just makes it last longer. Really, people need their friends and significant others to listen to them and support them when they get upset—not fix anything for them, just listen. The personal bond matters more than the venting. As I got better at shutting up and listening and letting people have their emotions, it became easier to express my own feelings, knowing that I wouldn't get throttled for it (or dismissed) like I did when I was a kid.

How are you at expressing your feelings? How do you handle it when other people express theirs? Do you even know *how* to feel sometimes? A dysfunctional childhood can make you good at shutting down your feelings, or having them imposed on you. Brian Fahey reminds us in *The Power of Balance* that, "It takes more energy to suppress feelings than to express them." Not containing your feelings doesn't mean squelching anger or complaining. It's about allowing yourself to feel what you're feeling and communicating your feelings appropriately. You have the right to do that. It can be challenging if you grew up with your feelings rejected, and kept them knotted up inside you. That becomes a recipe for social awkwardness, and even for developing diseases as you get older. (See chapter 17.)

When you grew up drenched in dramas, managing other people's emotions, there wasn't much room for your own feelings, maybe not even tolerance of them. Now, when you're in tricky emotional situations, the confusion doesn't come from lack of affect. You feel very deeply. But you may have developed the survival mechanism of ignoring your own feelings, believing no one else cares how you feel.

We're vulnerable when we express emotion. In some families, it means vulnerability to criticism, shaming, scorn, or attack. Was it safer to swallow your feelings? Did you learn the hard way that expressing feelings could make a bad situation worse? Did you often feel safe to express yourself as a kid? Keeping emotions bottled up has mental and physical consequences. If you've ever blown up unexpectedly or thrown a private fit when something embarrassed or frustrated you, you've experienced this. If your habit is not to deal with your feelings, they're eventually going to deal with you. And usually not conveniently.

I didn't shed a tear at either of my parents' funerals. I was there, and the loss was a bummer. I didn't make a conscious decision *not* to cry; it just didn't happen. But when it eventually did happen, the emotion caught me unaware. It was Christmas Eve, the week after I got married. My mother had passed about four months earlier, and my dad several years before that, so neither of my parents saw my wedding. My new bride and I were attending a traditional candlelight service. To conclude the service, everyone in the church got a candle. The lights were out, and we were all on our feet singing hymns while our candles burned. It was a nice Norman Rockwell scene. As I stood holding my candle, my mom came to mind. She was gone, and I had never really mourned the loss. Despite all the insanity in our house during my adolescence, at that moment I believed that she did love me. My sudden tears hit me like a stun gun. In that moment, it occurred to me that there was not one person left on earth who loved me, including, I feared, the woman standing next to me whom I had just married five days earlier! Several suppressed emotions ganged up on me at once and had to get out.

Despite what anyone taught you, you're allowed to have your feelings, and express them. When you start healing yourself, and living more *in spirit*, suppressed emotions won't catch up with you so easily. You'll deal with things more productively. You create and reaffirm an inner calm during your quiet "me time," and that will allow you to grow and thrive and succeed. Your private moments of mindful self-renewing will keep you connected to your goals and your Source.

9 RE-ORIENT, AND SHINE YOUR LIGHT

Not every "A-Ha! moment" we have is a happy one, but every one is important. They shake us out of ruts. They cause us to think differently or redirect our lives in some way. I had one of those moments many years ago, standing alone at a bus station in northern California one evening.

I was waiting to catch the airport shuttle to fly back home. I'd just completed another training in Hanna Somatics, a mind-body discipline. Earlier that day, my classmates talked about everything they were looking forward to getting back to. They were excited about seeing their significant others, their kids and their friends. All I knew was that I was going back to my little apartment in Philadelphia, back to my daily grind, with no one special eagerly awaiting my return.

It was Sunday evening, the bus station was closed, and since the airport shuttle wouldn't be there for another hour I waited outside. As it got dark, a row of overhead lights began to turn on automatically, lighting up one after another—plink...plink...plink. All except one. Five of the six lights popped on in sequence and were shining brightly at the station entrance, but that one light couldn't get going. It glimmered and faded, shining for a few seconds then flickering out. I paced back and forth for 45 minutes watching it, practically cheering for it. When it did plink on, it was as bright and brilliant as the other lights, but it had trouble getting started and couldn't stay lit.

I threw myself a pity party the rest of the night—I felt small, insignificant and depressed. That light had hit me with my reality. I was that light. I'd spent the last ten days with people who spoke of such interesting, meaningful lives—compared to how I saw my own. I felt they had what I wanted, but didn't know how to get. Thankfully, it was dark when the shuttle bus arrived, and no one could see this 40-something guy choking back tears and feeling sorry for himself all the way to the airport. That light had reminded me of who I thought I was at that time. I had the same good qualities as everyone else, but didn't know how to let my light shine. Most people sleep on red-eye flights; I was up all night, thinking about that light and how it resembled my life. Was that flickering bulb being only a small part of what it was created to be? Was I doing the same thing? Now you know what the bulb couldn't know—you can create a more fulfilling life story. You can shine your own light.

In spite of your past conditioning, you can build your self-esteem and know that you matter. You have a light within you to be discovered. (Of course, everybody has "low self-esteem" anymore, to the point that the term has lost a lot of meaning. If you really have low self-esteem, you know it.) You hold yourself back and often don't go after what or whom you really want. You don't always treat yourself very kindly. In a practical sense, self-esteem—like spirituality and your voice—is more of a verb than a noun. It influences what you do, and don't do.

To paraphrase UT professor Bob Solomon: "Self-esteem motivates you to become all you are, to be inspired by what you think and believe, and to act without fear." Healthy self-esteem gives you the poise and confidence to express your ideas and opinions—the way "normal people" do. Self-esteem allows you to see yourself as equal to others, regardless of their positions or titles. (I've worked with healthcare professionals in hospitals for years, and lemme tell you, some people's egos will try to run you over if your self-esteem flinches.) Your self-esteem directly influences your communication skills: the healthier your concept of yourself, the better a communicator you'll be, especially when someone challenges your ideas. If you haven't been comfortable or effective in arguing or debating points of view, it could be partly from not believing enough in yourself to express your thoughts confidently. But know this: **it's okay to ask for what you want and say what you think.** Just remember that staying calm, being kind, and having a sense of humor are more effective than sarcasm, defensiveness or hostility.

If you didn't learn to like yourself or believe in yourself, it's harder to go after what you want, or maybe even *know* what you want. That was our childhood reality. We often underestimate our capabilities and what we can become because of what we got, or missed. If you weren't encouraged to recognize and develop your potential as a child, you may lower your aspirations and risk accomplishing less as an adult. Since, as the proverb says, we can always see the other guy's hunchback, check this out:

I didn't go to college after high school. I was sure I didn't have the intellect for it. After all, my dad had told me for years that I was "without a doubt the *dumbest* thing!" And when I was a young kid attracted to a hobby or a sport, I often wasn't allowed to do it unless I could do it on my own. Some parents forget what it was like to be a kid, going in many directions as they try to discover who they are. To my parents, I was required to make anything I showed interest in my lifelong pursuit. The response I usually got was, "No... because you won't stick with it." Were you encouraged to fully explore your fascinations when you were young, to see what might inspire you or ignite a passion? Lots of luck, if pursuing multiple interests would have required parental support or assistance.

I had no clear direction after graduating high school. I fell into in a low-paying, dead-end job (with the stoners). After a few years, I found my way into broadcasting school and a nearly 13-year radio career. My determination was shaped by my martial arts training; I began going to the dojo every night when I was 15, mowing lawns and washing cars to pay for it myself. I developed self-discipline from the grounding, meditative practices that anchor martial arts. (If this sparks your interest and you choose to explore traditional classical karate or kung-fu, you'll see its benefit in your self-esteem, your self-discipline and your physical fitness.) Most traditional martial arts are taught as a way of life – a peaceful life, not just as fighting methods. You might also enjoy the various Eastern meditative practices. Most of them will fall right in line with becoming more spiritually oriented. With time and intention, you can allow your spiritual practice to become *your* way of life. You'll be inspired by the results.

Why have a simple spiritual practice? It will help you recognize the truth of your past, help you appreciate everything and everyone in your life now, and what you can create going forward. As you become who you choose to be, your inner light can shine brighter every day. Your family struggles and shames created your childhood—now you have the power to create a new truth. Seeing a new truth can be painful for some people. Be brave enough.

There's a mountain of hidden work behind anyone who grew up in painful, self-destroying homes. We had to work hard to appear "normal" to our friends and neighbors, teachers, and the other kids at school. It's how we protected ourselves from embarrassment and shame—by keeping the family problems hidden. I hope you don't know how it feels to be an absolute wreck inside, and need to put up a cool facade for everyone to see. I suspect you may.

I got to know many people in different towns as I moved in my radio career. In one city, I knew a young woman from a very affluent family. They were very visible in the community and members of the country club. The community didn't know that the father had serious anger issues, and he would frequently beat his daughter for any perceived mistake. She told me it wasn't uncommon just before the family headed out for an evening at the country club, where she and her siblings were expected to be perfect young ladies and gentlemen. This continued all the way into her early 20s. Some people from dysfunctional families can display polished social skills, but can struggle in intimate relationships. This is a well-known reality. In my friend's case, she wound up in a support group trying to work out her troubles with the men she chose as boyfriends – men who had personalities like her father's. And yes, one boyfriend hit her.

No one wants their family's "dirty laundry" made public. Sometimes the family forces us to keep secrets; some of us lie about our personal realities, even to ourselves. We want people to think we're "normal" and that we come from a good family, that our lives are as balanced and rewarding as those of our peers.

When I finally got fully out on my own, working in radio in another part of the country, I used a stage name. (I said it was to protect my anonymity, but maybe it was because I desperately wanted to be someone besides who I thought I was back then.) No one knew me, so I could invent a totally different person. I made up things to tell people, things I could be proud of, things that would sound "normal." That worked a little, but not as much as I'd hoped—the knowledge and skills I needed to make it believable weren't going to just magically appear. It's true that you take yourself with you wherever you go. No matter what I may have wanted, I was still the same guy who came from "other than normal."

I lied my ass off anyway, telling people what I wanted them to think about me. In truth, I didn't go to college until I was 30, but I wanted the people I met to think I was educated like they were. The truth was too embarrassing to me. German philosopher Nietzsche understood this, even back in the 1800s. He said if a child was brought up in "complicated domestic circumstances," it's just as natural for him to lie to serve his interests as tell the truth. "He lies in all innocence."

83

It's not necessarily better to block out your unpleasant memories or deny your childhood reality. Revising it and creating a different narrative may give you happier memories, but everyone who knew you then—and a creeping feeling way down inside—can pop up unexpectedly to force reality back onto you. We all know people whose lives aren't nearly as wonderful and exciting as their social media posts suggest, but if it helps them feel better, God bless them. However, there's another direction to take.

Rejecting your past experience is not always denial. Some people really do get on with their lives. In the field of Positive Psychology, the heady term for this is a "salutogenic orientation." It means focusing on your strengths and favorable qualities, and building them. That's the opposite of giving your energy to problems and always trying to fix whatever you feel is broken. If the truth is too uncomfortable, find the strength to focus on any positives, rather than deny your experience.

Identifying the scars left by your childhood experience is the first step in successful re-orienting. When you are willing to recognize the after-effects of your childhood, you can start making healthier, more thoughtful life choices and nurturing your own self-esteem. You can see where you are in this process by how comfortable or uncomfortable it makes you. Deniers would rather have the work done *for* them, or not at all. Re-orienters are willing to do the work.

Re-orienting yourself is not necessarily a process with quick results. I'd never learned how to be a "normal" kid, so becoming a "normal" adult was going to time and work. It took years to shed teenage-level emotions and thought processes.

Even if you've identified the source of your pain, one goal is to remember that you are so much more than "an adult child from a dysfunctional family." Can you see yourself as spirit, light, a soul with human form? You can shape your life any way you choose. You have amazing things to accomplish. For example, think about all the things you can do with your voice: laugh, sound effects, funny character voices and accents, singing in a dozen different musical styles. One of the reasons we can do vocal stunts is that the space between our vocal cords and our lips has so much flexibility. You can deliberately shape your resonating space to achieve your intended sound or sound quality. Please notice the metaphor: you can do that with your life, too. You can intentionally shape how you feel and act by considering new ideas and different approaches. You can become the individual you aspire to be, without worrying about others' opinions about whether you're "normal." No one deserves to feel that they have to lie about themselves to feel "normal" or as worthy as anybody else. If you received a not-too-concealed message from your family—that you were of little value—consider that no kid should ever to have to feel that way.

Discovering your own inner light isn't easy if you've been hung up on cultural norms. My generation—late baby boomer, born in the mid-1960s, with Depression-era parents—saw conformity stressed. We were often taught not to stand out, but to be like everyone else. Were you ever told, "Don't call attention to yourself, or Don't make a scene?"

Dysfunctional families play by their own rules. Unfortunately, what happens in Vegas, doesn't always stay in Vegas. You might have been able to hide some things to keep up appearances, but you probably didn't have any control over your family's issues. These may have occasionally spilled out into the neighborhood, or humiliated you in front of your friends. Several of my childhood memories, and possibly some of yours, include mortifying scenes in restaurants, shopping centers, and in front of our house—in my case, sometimes with police cars present.

When you're a powerless kid growing up in a powder keg, you learn to do whatever you can to keep the fuse from being lit. Sometimes it works, other times, there's a scene.

The result of always trying to placate others, of desperately trying to calm things down, is developing the personality of an appeaser—giving up part of yourself to try to keep the peace. I often did whatever I could to keep smoldering tempers from turning into five-alarm blazes. Were you treated as unfit or inferior? The result? You were trained to take the blame for things that aren't your responsibility. The light within you dimmed.

That was the past. Now you can re-orient to a new reality. Adjusting your intention, visualizing, spirituality, and aspiring to become more like What you came from will let you see that your inner light has never gone out.

Re-orient by starting small, and keep it simple. What inspires you? What are you passionate about? What brings you joy, and vaults you into "the zone?" How do you turn 'unfulfilled you' into what you really want to be? If your childhood experience pushed you into patterns that hinder you, you might have been made very self-protecting. And you might not have realized you were trapped in that pattern.

All the way into my late thirties, I reflexively protected myself—rarely reaching out to anyone to let them know me. I was hesitant and felt socially unskilled. I felt unable to create the happy, three-dimensional life that I thought my peers were leading. We all cope in our individual ways, growing up in tense, erratic homes. In my house, my sister and I were opposite sides of the same coin: she often acted *out*, while I retreated *in*. Neither of us was a typical teenager, and we ran with completely different crowds. She found her 'family' in the partying, wrong company crowd as a teenager; for me, it was studying martial arts and reading Eastern philosophy. My life was a Simon and Garfunkel lyric: "I have my books and my poetry to protect me. I am shielded in my armor." After several years, I was lucky to find something I was passionate about, something to counterbalance the madness of my home. If you didn't discover your outlet when you were young, create yours Now.

There are scores of talented people whose creative or athletic abilities began in difficult, even tragic family conditions, maybe as an offset to their suffering. If that's part of your story, keep going. Whether you know it or not, there are without question many creative sides to you. Want proof? If you weren't creative and resourceful, you never would have made it this far and outlasted your family's dysfunction. You are an artist. Express your artistry, on your own behalf and every day. See your life as an artistic journey. It will be exhilarating. And you've earned it.

When we're young, we define ourselves by what we're told. Going through puberty develops us more than just physically— we undergo much cognitive and emotional development until our mid-twenties. These foundations influence the people we'll become and the life choices we'll make. Sometimes, our choices confine us in listless patterns that we don't realize. Author Paul Pearsall describes this as "languishing rather than truly thriving." (His book, *The Beethoven Factor*, is freakin' awesome!) If we're trained to keep ourselves safe and shielded at an early age, it interferes with the fulfilling lives we're meant to lead. But with some determined re-orienting, a different reality awaits us.

This book isn't about getting over anything, it's about getting *on,* to the creative, exceptional life you were born for. If you give the people around you the things that make you feel good, multiply the good deed and let *yourself* have those things! That's not selfish! Dysfunctional families are created by adults who put *their* wants and needs first. Their kids are often told they're wrong or selfish, because they're not granting the parent's wish.

Psychologist William James wrote, "That which we are, we shall teach, not voluntarily but involuntarily." If you grew up marinating in others' self-indulgent behavior, what do you think you learned?

Being self-focused isn't always negative; sometimes it's necessary, possibly even life-saving. One recipe for a dysfunctional family is having the people at the top make sure their personal, emotional and chemical needs are met, with little regard for what this does to their kids. When those at the top don't have their needs met, they raise hell in confusing or frightening ways. This kind of acting out can sometimes engender acting in—one causes harm, the second can be used to *protect from* harm. Are you ready to realize, **the real world is not what your family was?** The behaviors you learned don't necessarily fit the life you lead now. If traits like empathy, humanitarianism and social consciousness weren't modeled for you or taught to you, consider learning them now, like volunteering or giving to charities, for example.

On reflection, you may find that your response to selfishness is the opposite: becoming other-oriented, giving a great deal of yourself. This might be another form of self-protection, or a way to feel that something you do matters. Many people do volunteer work or other altruistic activities, or end up in helping professions. Do you take care of others more than you take care of yourself?

We learned to protect ourselves in ways that worked for us. (I was studying martial arts by age 15; I'd already been practicing 'self-defense' for years.) Now as an adult, some people who don't know us well might judge our self-protective ways as selfish. As they see us more and know us better, it becomes clearer whether the problem is our self-protection or their judgment.

If that's been true for you, recognize that you can stop defending yourself. Let your light shine by sharing the best part of yourself with others. Medical research confirms that sharing joy promotes health. When you create your own joy, you can share it with others.

We've agreed on the concept; here's your recipe. Do one thing every day that you love and that you're good at. Let it put you in your best mood. It could be simple and direct, like riding your bike or listening to your favorite music. You could choose a longer-term goal, like working towards a degree, or making progress on a creative project. If sitting quietly and meditating is your thing, do that. Your choices are endless. Find your bliss, enjoy it and share it. That lets your light shine from the inside out.

The joyful moments you give to yourself will last longer when you involve others, even in small ways. Give someone a compliment. Let them ahead of you in line at the grocery store. Pay for coffee, or even a meal, for someone in uniform, and thank them for what they do. Some call this 'paying it forward', but you're really paying yourself as well. It feels good to put a smile on someone's face and make their day better. Ralph Waldo Emerson advised: "To know even one life has breathed easier because you have lived – that is to have succeeded."

We all get caught up in commitments and responsibilities, and put off doing the things that energize us. Being "all business" can stick us in a rut. Getting used to that pattern can feel like "survival mode." But we don't have to become statistics.

Sociology professors teach that most of us stay pretty much the same throughout our lives. Academic studies show that when we get into our 70s, 80s and 90s, we're older versions of the selves we've always been. Is that what you want? You can keep getting better. Stagnation sucks. Now that you know better, you deserve to shine, and the light within you was put there with Divine purpose. Doubting that only indulges your negativity. You can stop defeating yourself at the same time you can let others see you shine. Joy and passion are contagious. Others will want to "catch it" from you.

10 PUT ON SOME CYNDI LAUPER, FOR FUN

Think a minute: When you were a kid, did you have fun the way the other kids did? Did you have to be always on alert, nervous whenever you heard a certain tone of voice or saw a certain facial expression? "Fun" may have been defined differently at your house—your kid-fun may have felt more like a temporary break from the anxiety, chaos, pain, or shame.

Your childhood might still be shaping you. You can't have the same attitude as others, if you grew up being the caretaker, referee, or scapegoat. How about your present-day fun? Do you give yourself permission to cut loose and let go? It might not be comfortable for you to relax and become vulnerable. Or are you concerned about having "too much fun?" Not building healthy bonding, trust and rapport with your parents left you more susceptible to peer pressure and even harmful influence. If you didn't hear rational grown-ups' voices when you were faced with drinking, smoking, drugs, and sex as a teenager, the "fun" you had might have led you to a host of troubles, and you may not have those voices still.

You take your old conditioning with you wherever you go. You can't leave it on the dresser, like your wallet or sunglasses. It will affect the quality of your "fun;" if you're too busy watching for anything that might hurt or embarrass you, you won't be fully open to the people and conditions around you. Trying to control your surroundings can cost you socially. Either you won't have as good a time as you'd like, or you could unintentionally push people away—what if they want to include you in their fun?

Picture the dance floor at a wedding reception. Many men can't dance well, but they're willing to overcome their self-consciousness and give it a try, to keep their dates or partners happy. That didn't used to be me. I've had women practically dislocate their arms, trying to pull me out of a chair to dance. My old conditioning didn't want me to look silly, but my reluctance was more than that. The training I took from my childhood home wouldn't let me lower my shields and let people see me doing something uninhibited. Being seen dancing was too far outside the boundaries I'd set for self-protecting ME.

If you grew up powerless in an out of control place, it's fair to expect adult issues of control. That doesn't always mean controlling other people, often it's about staying in control of your circumstances and guarding yourself.

Throughout my 20s, at parties, ballgames, or concerts, I always paid close attention to how many drinks everyone else had. I monitored the environment like it was my job. I'd often remind someone, "That's your third beer, man." You can imagine how much fun I was at a party. I was uncomfortable around people who were drinking, having grown up with the disastrous effects of parents who drank. I did the only thing I could to maintain some control, but that wasn't a formula for fun—for others, or for me. Trying to prevent disaster kept me in chronic self-protection mode, and none of us enjoyed it. Through high school and my early 20s, I protected myself at social gatherings by giving myself a role. I would either cling to whoever I knew best, hide in a corner, or help serve food, or clean up. I wasn't anti-social. I was glad to be with everyone, but I protected myself by becoming less accessible, by taking myself out of the game. Friends I grew up with say they barely remember me being involved in several things we experienced together; I was often such a low-profile presence that having fun my way meant disappearing to others.

Understand that you're allowed to have fun, and you can enjoy yourself. The good people in your life want you to. There's no rulebook that determines what's fun and how you should show it. It's okay if you experience fun differently from those around you, as long as you're not disruptive or upsetting. You don't have to be the life of the party—there are always others willing to play that role. You'll know you're having fun when you feel fully present in the moment and getting positive response from those around you. At first you may need to observe your emotions intellectually, because dysfunctional families are so much about anger, commotion, anxiety, guilt, and feeling let down. This might be new for you, but unless you're an arsonist or an axe murderer, have faith. You can have fun. Remember also to allow others the latitude for their brands of fun.

You can harness new energy and reverse old, restrictive attitudes that were conditioned into you. Your outlook can change. Social situations won't be intimidating. In my case, I stopped trying to play "hall monitor" and being concerned with everyone behaving themselves the way I thought they should. It became easier to fully participate and enjoy the moment. This is a work in progress, too, but it's very satisfying.

Expressing "your fun" differently doesn't make your experience any less legitimate. Sitting in movie theatres, concert halls or ballparks nearly expressionless while everyone around you is laughing or cheering, doesn't mean you're not having a great time. Soaking up the good vibes feels great. You don't need to impress anybody. True friends and good people should accept you as you are once *YOU* accept yourself, without apology. Obviously, personal styles vary. Behaving like an introvert is one option, but so is the opposite, and some people go too far to either extreme. (Either way, thinking before speaking is always a good idea.) If you're pushing so hard to have fun that you go too far and behave inappropriately, nobody has fun. Being too much of a smartass, or at inappropriate times, can grate on others. In fact, being "too quiet" can be less irritating than rubbing others noses in your intellect.

If you need a reason to thank your dysfunctional home, some kids from dysfunctional families are extremely astute, creative and academically accomplished—possibly because they had to be, to satisfy parental demands or to escape their families. Sometimes, people raised in cruel environments earn advanced degrees and become very successful professionally because that was their escape. But academic success doesn't necessarily translate into social success.

In the 1980s, Harvard psychologist Howard Gardner developed the theory that we have multiple intelligences. These include logical-mathematical intelligence, visual-spatial intelligence, musical intelligence, and several others. Interpersonal intelligence is also on that list; we could also call it social intelligence. The theory is that everyone has a portion of each type of intelligence, but we're most dominant in one or two. Social intelligence is the center, around which we rate our other "intelligences." We're judged by others in how we present ourselves socially. We all need a good social filtering system to be successful. Some don't use their filters as well as others.

We've all met people who can't seem to stop trying to prove they were the smartest in the room. They act like know-it-alls, correcting others, trying to come off as well-informed, spouting as if they understand everything better than everyone else. I've watched group moderators try to rein these people in, and lose people because of a spout-off jerk. Brilliant doesn't necessarily mean socially brilliant, and your social intelligence tells people more about you than your IQ score. Be mindful that your brand of fun doesn't send others an unintended message.

Some personalities don't mesh. If it's not easy to have fun around certain people, you can still be kind, because you're you, not because they're them. If someone is acting conceited or obnoxious, remember that it's not about you. Carlos Castaneda quotes Don Juan: "Self-importance is merely self-pity in

95

disguise." Hold onto that. Because we learned to blame ourselves for other people's crap, letting someone's snooty behavior be his or her own problem takes some effort; but because everything gets easier with practice, the emotional burdens that came with you from your childhood can be unloaded. With attention, self-esteem, fun and true happiness won't be out of reach.

Abraham Lincoln is quoted: "Most folks are as happy as they make up their minds to be." Even if he wasn't the first person to express this, he might be the most familiar. The truth is, we can be free to choose, to be happy or anything else. Please note: authenticity is vital. Some people can make themselves miserable working to be happy. Or they might put on a fake happy attitude *because* they're miserable.

Some people take "happy" and "fun" to dangerous depths, whether thoughtlessly or as another way to escape the distress of home. This doesn't necessarily refer to adrenaline-rush activities like bungee jumping or Extreme Sports; it's more about self-abusive behaviors like binge drinking, drug abuse, reckless sexual activities, or motorcycle stunts in traffic. A devil-may-care attitude may be "fun" in the moment, and amusing to watch, but it can be terribly costly. Remember the line from The Who's song, *My Generation*: "I hope I die before I get old." Sadly, sometimes they get their wish, and we see them at their funerals instead of in the prime of their lives. How many young celebrities never reached the age of 30? Go ahead, name three, who had all the money and fame we wish we had. Worse, sometimes the untimely death happens to someone they've influenced with their brand of "fun." As they used to say on the old Dragnet TV series: "The stories you are about to hear are true. The names were changed to protect the innocent."

In my early 20s, I worked with Derek and Andy in different roles at a printing company. Derek was in his mid-20s, lifted weights and took steroids to bulk up, tattooed on every body part we could see, boasting about staying up all night partying with booze and cocaine. He used to brag that he had no plans to live past the age of 40—"Have you ever seen anybody over 40 who's happy?" He maintained he was an adult and free to make his own choices. Andy, another of our co-workers, was in his 50s at the time. Derek would often tease him and tell him he needed to get out more and have fun because Derek felt Andy's life was dull. We all knew that Andy was the caregiver for his chronically ill wife; he'd leave the shop a couple of times a day to run home and then come back. Derek nagged Andy until they finally went out one night to the track, planning to bet on the horses, have a couple of beers and watch the races. Derek brought his cocaine with him that night and told us he talked Andy into trying it. Several weeks later, the two of them went out again. Neither of them showed up for work the next day. Later, we got word that Andy had died. We never saw Derek again. We still don't know what happened to him. The conclusion we came to at the time was that Derek's "fun" got Andy killed.

It's a cautionary tale: Sometimes danger comes from a connection two or three links away. Fast forward 20 years. Kurt and I had mutual friends, but we'd only see each other when the group got together. He was an electrician, but I couldn't understand how he got any work done. I never saw him without a drink in his hand—apparently, he couldn't have fun unless alcohol was involved. He would always sneak in a flask, even when we went to see *The Passion of the Christ*! He'd often badger me about "not being a man" because I wasn't a whiskey-drinking, cigar-smoking, outdoorsy person who hunted and fished.

Regina acted as the social director of our group. One year, when she and her husband planned a Halloween party, I said I didn't want to go if Kurt would be there. I said I would be uncomfortable because Kurt didn't like me. Regina's response was, "It's not that he dislikes you, he just thinks you don't know how to have fun." She was the long-time friend of Kurt's girlfriend, so possibly she didn't wasn't to risk that relationship. She actually helped enable his drinking and his treatment of me. Eventually, I moved to another city and lost touch with most of the group. What I remember is how Kurt worked so hard to prove how cool he was by masking his alcohol dependence as "having fun." If we had been friends, I would worry, because that kind of behavior usually has an expiration date.

Both Derek and Kurt defined "having fun" in ways we would define as "abusing their bodies." It might be those attitudes came from behavior that was modeled for them in childhood, or judgements that were laid on them as they were growing up. It could have been adolescent behavior that continued because there weren't consequences. Could living unrestrained lifestyles have been their definition of "living life to the fullest?" Since addiction tendencies often run in families, could it be that they were genetically pre-disposed, and each defined "freedom" as not having to follow any rules? We can't know, we can only observe the results.

As an adult, it's your job to make decisions aligned with social norms, local and federal laws, and an awareness of the people around you. If you think it's fun to tap dance naked, you can—in the privacy of your own home. As Oliver Wendell Holmes Jr. said, "The right to swing my arms in any direction ends where your nose begins." So, you are as free as you can be, until you impose on others' freedom. It was selfish of Derek to insist that Andy have fun Derek's way. It was possibly disastrous for Andy to give in. In Kurt's world, not being like him means being wrong. He had the right to disapprove of me, and I have the right to disagree with him, as long as we both had manners.

Please be assured, if you're not having "fun" the way the people around you seem to be, go ahead and have fun as you define it—as long as you're not interfering with anyone else's fun. If she isn't already, make Cyndi Lauper your mantra. Her 80's hit, "Girls Just Wanna Have Fun" championed wild looks, unconventional hair colors, and explained or excused a lot of unconventional behaviors. What you may not know is something she shared in an interview: in her pre-celebrity days, disapproving kids used to throw rocks at her, but she dared to be who she was, anyway. Cyndi Lauper was not destined to be common. She was exceptional; but just as important, she dared to be true to who she is. She showed a generation of young women that they could defy convention, have their own "fun" and be uniquely themselves. So, if she isn't already, let Cyndi Lauper be your inspiration.

Your life is for you, and anyone you invite into it. Who cares if it doesn't Instagram well? You don't have to apologize for not being part of what "the herd" thinks is all right.

Ever go to a traditionally-trained acupuncturist? They sometimes refer to heavy terms like "external pernicious influence." Let me clue you in, so you can impress your friends with your knowledge. That's one of the principles of Traditional Chinese Medicine, and refers to the outside forces that bombard our minds and bodies and cause emotional, mental and physical symptoms. Application to our young lives? You bet. Growing up in dysfunctional families, we were constantly bombarded with those pernicious influences. If young, developing personalities evolve in a disordered system, the ways we understand and relate to the world become disordered too.

When we grow up coping with tension, anxiety and others' hysterics, the mindset and behaviors we develop in it become hardwired into us. You wouldn't be wrong to call it "neuropsychological malware," if you want to use a computer term. Unless we can upheave the upheaval and practice different approaches and behaviors, our minds will continue to operate in the ways they were trained, long after childhood is gone. We have to guess what "normal" is, because we most often were trained in its opposite.

Here's how it all works: Our brains are basically pattern generators. The nerve cells "learn" to fire in certain ways in response to our repeated daily experiences. These neural firing patterns become our feelings, reactions and behaviors. Those learned patterns won't change until you change them; that change happens because of will, intention, and focused, persistent desire and awareness. The best way to "get out from under it" is to acknowledge, take over and own it – both the problem and the solution. The thinking, feeling and behavior patterns we developed growing up become set as the default. (Want the scientific verbiage? They're managed by the subcortical, involuntary portions of the brain, without your conscious awareness.) Translation: you have to want a change, and be aware of that want, to evolve. You must recognize, then take over, your automatic reflexes and replace them with deliberate thinking responses. You can "overwrite" the programs parked in your subconscious by thoughtfully clicking into your voluntary brain centers. Changing your response patterns will change your behavior, and once you've made the effort to change the response patterns, no other effort is even needed.

This is what academics and professionals call neuroplasticity. It's the proven theory that brain cells adjust and reorganize themselves, and re-assign functions, if we stimulate them in new ways. (Remember the movie *Field of Dreams*? If you build it, they will come.) We can heal and change our brains, and thereby change our lives. Want to sound like a neuroscience researcher? "Neurons that fire together wire together." Mind-body practice teachers say this all the time. Neuroplasticity has been understood since the 1940s; physical and occupational therapists, neuropsychologists, cognitive behavioral therapists, *and* clinical vocologists have jobs because of it. Now that you've been introduced to it, you can help yourself: using deliberate, conscious control over the unconscious habits you want to change is as simple as resetting the reflex that pops up when the habit pops up. (Didn't say "Totally easy," but it IS simple.) Engaging your higher brain centers—the intentional parts—can reset the default, and you're on your way to Exceptional.

No need to feel defensive. Nobody is saying your brain is abnormal. There's no pathology, just a mismatch between a "normal childhood" and the one we got. Our home environments trained us differently, so our emotional wiring and processing operate differently. The good news is, our brains are changeable. The *great* news is, you can be your own tech support, remove the "virus" and re-write your software—through intention, and conscious, deliberate behavior.

Rehab professionals apply neuroplasticity principles every day, as they help people recover from injuries, strokes or surgery. You can use the same principles in your daily life. You don't need rehab; you didn't lose something you need to regain. You're building new talents and skills, gaining better development of some important processes. You grow by trying out new behaviors and affirming new thoughts that come out of your deliberate intentions. You have to want it; so study, learn, and practice. If you're consistent, you'll see change. The brain starts making new and different connections, and more importantly, lets go of the old ones that no longer serve you. Don't laugh, neuroscientists call it "pruning." You can call it "virus removal!"

You can literally rewire your brain. The difficulties and frustrations you've faced as an adult, coming out of a powerless childhood, can be remedied. It doesn't happen overnight, but it happens. Your childhood programming will have less and less influence over time. You'll become more empowered, and your life will start blossoming. It may feel a bit strange at first, because the "schedule" is off. I felt like I experienced my teenage years in my twenties, then did my twenties in my thirties. If you have those feelings, too, don't lament, rejoice! You're experiencing everything you want and need, and the timing doesn't affect the value.

How exactly do you rewire your brain to change the way it works? The short answer is, just do it. Go out into your everyday world and look for opportunities to practice living the life you want, the way you want to live it. Be the YOU you really are—whatever you visualize during your "me time." Remember that even small changes can make way for big effects. Act on your visualizations in any chance you can. Do it now. No positive change is too small.

When patients go through voice rehabilitation, they learn that any verbal exchange is an opportunity to practice using their real voice, the one they've been working to re-discover and develop. Let's do what they do, in our own daily exchanges. Wherever you are, whomever you're talking to, every situation presents the chance to put your vision into real practice. Keep it simple. We all have daily routines, so every day you can pick two or three routine occasions to intentionally practice being who you really want to be. The old saying is that you take yourself with you wherever you go. Try bringing a new self—the YOU that you're purposely creating—into a few of your routine encounters every day. Spot these opportunities and use them. See that they can start influencing your other interactions.

Want an example? Let's say you're not a morning person. When you walk into work, put on a cheerful expression and be deliberately upbeat. If someone asks the routine question "How are you?" answer them with an energetic "I am fantastic!" (It's not a lie detector, just a choice to put out new energy.) See how it draws a good response. Then, keep that enthusiasm going; it makes everyone's day better, starting with yours. If you know you're going to be in a situation that calls for a little more formality, then give yourself the "assignment" ahead of time (even if it's only few minutes before) to slow down and consider your words carefully, to make good eye contact and be a good listener. Take your "I Am" statement out of your pocket (remember chapter 6) and look at it. *Be* what you wrote.

If you're invited to a happy hour or some work-related function, decide in advance to practice something different than your past habit/s. If that habit is introvert, maybe you can allow yourself to be a little more outgoing and sociable. Don't try to completely change who are, just be willing to experiment and explore, and maybe expand your horizons, especially if you're tired of having to deflect comments that "you're so quiet." Engage with people, show a genuine interest in them, do your best to keep a smile on. If you've usually been on the other end of the scale, more socially forceful, then you can practice backing off and letting others take the lead. Slightly "out of your comfort zone" (your default habit) is where the best action is. With a little planning and some practice, you can choreograph a satisfying day. When you see how well it works, you'll want to keep doing it.

Meaningful change begins in our ordinary moments. Opportunities to practice being the YOU you want to be arise all day. Sometimes I would practice when just walking down the street. Philadelphia is a great walking town, which offered me several daily "practice sessions." When running a quick errand, or walking to the train station, I could make better eye contact with people, give them a smile, a "Good morning!" or just a friendly nod. Go for a walk and try it. See what a win-win it is. It can seem challenging if you've felt uncomfortable or shy in the past; but that's why you practice—in low-risk opportunities—with intention. It will make a noticeable difference. Practice with the attitude of "I can do" rather than "I don't want to do." It's not work, it's a fun, creative experiment.

When working with people who need to improve their diets and health, nutritionists don't simply say stop eating this or that. Telling someone what *not* to do doesn't empower or inspire healthful change. Good nutritionists advise adding in the better stuff: non-processed, organic whole foods, more nutrient-dense and locally grown fruits and vegetables. Old-school lifeguards would say, "out with the bad, in with the good." In this case, it's "in with the good, to push out the bad." The better alternatives steadily replace the less-healthy stuff. The way to wellness is paved with learning and consistently practicing better eating habits, and noticing the results. (More about the value of great nutrition coming in chapter 17.) This is a practice to apply to more than how we eat. We can make new choices, to replace the habits developed when we were too young and too overwhelmed by family drama to be aware of the habits we were developing.

105

Now, if you're deliberate and consistent with new behaviors, you can train your brain to start developing new pathways and making new connections. You're not trying to re-invent the wheel, just change your trajectory to move toward a more satisfying life.

Psychologist Jeremy Dean in his book *Making Habits, Breaking Habits*, tells us that we need at least 21 days of purposeful practice to create a simple habit. More complex habits take a lot longer. You'll need consistency to change your thoughts and behaviors. Create practice sessions in common activities, doing familiar things with a new twist. Productive change doesn't happen by telling yourself to stop doing something but to *start* doing something, to choose a different idea and make it a daily action.

Vocal therapists work with a lot of schoolteachers—voice problems are an occupational hazard, because the job requires them to be vocal athletes. And in a former life I spent more than a dozen years as a radio disc jockey then promotion director. Teachers and broadcasters have something in common with several other professions: they're never really "off duty." Educators are always on the lookout for things they can use in the classroom—materials, experiences, observations, etc. This is true for on-air radio personalities, too. They're always keenly observant for something relatable and interesting to bring to their shows. Alter your brain circuitry. Put your inner teacher or radio personality to work for you, and see yourself move beyond the long-term ill effects left by your dysfunctional upbringing.

Your homework is simple: Start approaching some old things in new ways. You can intentionally exercise more positive and healthful thought patterns *and* actions in any routine encounter. Nothing will be perfect; it doesn't need to be. It's not about "getting it right." It's seeing the value of daily practice, changing how you respond to modern life and its challenges.

When drivers do something stupid or rude in traffic, for example, just let them. It's over and done; you're okay. Swearing or giving them the finger doesn't undo what they did and only raises your own blood pressure. Letting negative energy surge through you does not equal success. Or let's say your significant other is angry because you forgot to do something. Let him or her be upset. Apologize, admit you blew it, make amends if you can, whatever is necessary. Then let your partner get over it, instead of defensively returning fire and escalating the situation. You can start moving from *dysfunctional* to *Exceptional*, no matter how your childhood environment trained you. Your brain, and your life, is waiting for the chance.

12 KEEP YOUR EYES ON THE HORIZON

Some years ago, on a Monday morning, one of the nurses I worked with told me, "I saw you at the movie theater this weekend. I knew it was you because you always walk with your head down." Ouch. She was just making a casual observation; it wasn't a slam, but it got my attention. Anytime we see someone who looks familiar but they're too far away to see clearly, there are other ways to recognize them—how they dress, or the style of their hair, but also the way they sit, stand and move. Our posture and movement characteristics are the most visible parts of our personalities. The way I carried myself was an unfavorable marker of my inner world for a long time. How does this fit with your reality? The way you live in your body reflects who you are. Give it some thought; you could discover something about yourself.

"Eyes on the horizon" was the advice given to me by one of my teachers during Somatics training, coaching me on healthful posture and head-neck-spine alignment. It's a surprising game-changer, applied to everyday life. There are more benefits than you think. Holding your head properly upright sends a different message—you look better, for starters. A slumped-over, too-forward head looks like pain or despair; a head fully atop an upright spine, with eyes on the horizon, looks healthy, confident and approachable. Walking with a head-down posture closes you off and puts an approachability barrier between you and others. The more you can practice a healthy, head-up posture, the more the world opens to you. This may sound like a big result from such a minor change, but you might be surprised. *Chaos Theory* author James Gleick suggests that "Small perturbations in one's daily trajectory can have large consequences."

Introducing even a small variation in your daily behavior, consistently, changes the overall pattern and exerts powerful effects on how others respond to you. "Eyes on the horizon" practice is a direct application of what the previous chapter was all about. Patients working to heal vocal cord lesions are told, "We're not trying to re-invent the wheel, just alter the current trend that led to the injury. Your voice will start to get better because you've made the necessary adjustments." The graph below illustrates the nature of progress.

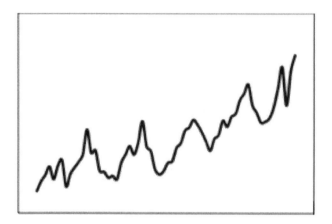

Progress is the same for vocal or any other behaviors. There will be successes as well as stumbles (peaks and valleys) but a general upward trend toward the goal. The goal here is to consistently practice a habit of upright posture—and experiencing its benefits. Keeping your head up increases your participation in the world around you and invites people in. If you carry yourself in a way that doesn't let you make eye contact, you won't be viewed as a warm friendly person, and others won't feel comfortable extending themselves toward you. A quick adjustment, and you're more accessible.

You may also notice that with regular, mindful practice of "eyes on the horizon" you start to feel livelier, more energized and engaging. Even subtle changes in your outer appearance can cause significant changes on the inside. Cosmetic surgeons have noticed this phenomenon in patients who get Botox injections in their facial muscles: taking away the wrinkles helps take away depression. Possibly if you're physically unable to frown, the brain starts to adjust and change its neurochemistry. But you don't have to get Botox injections and make payments on some plastic surgeon's boat to see these results. Just keep your head up to reap the benefits. In classical singing training, the idea of the noble or regal posture is often taught; staying fully upright keeps the working parts of your vocal mechanism in their best working position. This also makes a difference with your everyday speaking voice, promoting a brighter more energetic tone. A healthfully upright posture—not stiff and rigid, just comfortably "up"—can make an enormous difference. Test it. If your habit is to carry yourself with your head down and make limited eye contact with others, pick your head up and participate. Practice, and keep practicing. You will notice the difference. Your facial expression will soften, and you will seem like a friendlier person.

Human communication experts tell us that our body language reveals nonverbally much more than the words we speak. "Eyes on the horizon" changes what you say without uttering a word. Since your head is always on, you have plenty of opportunities every day to practice. I started by picking two specific times each day to be mindful and to deliberately keep my eyes on the horizon. Some mornings, for example, I would stop at Starbucks on the way to work and make the entire ritual a practice session: get off the train, walk over to the place, wait in line, order, get my drink, and complete my walk to work. All that while keeping my head up and putting a brighter, more lively expression on my face, instead of the drooped, sullen face that was my usual habit at 6:30 in the morning. I started getting different responses— smiles from other people coming and going, friendly greetings in the corridors; the baristas started greeting me by name instead of saying "decaf tall soy skinny mocha" as soon as they saw me.

You can practice "eyes on the horizon" anywhere: walking through the grocery store, riding the subway, sitting in the waiting room at the dentist's office, and on and on. You choose where and when, but choose regularly and in a variety of places. It's subtle, it's simple, and only you know you're doing it. You'll notice its value sooner than you think, and you'll remind yourself to do it more. Regular practice of "eyes on the horizon" helped me change my experience, and if you can make it a new behavior of your own, don't be surprised to hear things like "There's something different about you" from the people in your life.

If you need a postural change, it will take a little effort and concentration because of the way our sensory-motor system works. It takes time to acclimate to a new set of physical sensations. Our bodies and brains get used to the way we do things, especially our posture and movement patterns. They're automatic and don't require any conscious thought. The sensory-motor part of the brain doesn't know whether our posture and alignment patterns are healthful or harmful, it just does what we've trained it to do over time. Changing patterns takes attention and determination. Be patient with yourself. Let it evolve, and let yourself get used to new sensory awareness, even if it feels strange at first. Movement re-education pioneer F. Mathias Alexander wrote a statement in the middle of the last century that sums it up nicely:

One of the most remarkable of man's characteristics is his capacity for becoming used to conditions of almost any kind, whether good or bad, both in the self and in the environment, and once he has become used to such conditions they seem to him both right and natural. This capacity is a boon when it enables him to adapt himself to conditions which are desirable, but it may prove a great danger when the conditions are undesirable. When his sensory appreciation is so untrustworthy, it is possible for him to become so familiar with seriously

112

harmful conditions of misuse of himself that these malconditions will feel right and comfortable.

We could spend a long time considering Alexander's words—they refer to a lot more than postural habits. For now, know that your posture and body alignment is maintained by active muscles. Those muscles send information back into the brain so the signals to maintain the muscular contractions keep coming. It's an ongoing feedback loop. How you look when you sit in a chair, stand in an elevator, and walk down the street is maintained by your brain responding to sensations received from your body. The brain and the muscles cooperate and set a pattern. Whether that's a healthful, head-up, self-assured posture or a slumped over, head down, no eye contact, I-have-low-self-esteem posture is up to you. The sensory-motor parts of the brain are not "thinking" parts, so whatever pattern they're trained to generate, they'll accept as perfectly normal. When your childhood environment doesn't teach you to value yourself very much, you develop patterns that become obstacles to a confident, content appearance. Whether you're consciously aware of your posture habits or not, start deliberately keeping your eyes on the horizon, and notice what else changes.

As a Hanna Somatic Educator, working with people who have chronic tensions and aches/pains, I've seen how the body is a good storage container for all kinds of trauma. Many body-centered authors and educators teach that the various traumatic events of our lives are literally "recorded" in our bodies; and they can manifest as problems of posture and body alignment. We can develop habitual muscle tension patterns that result in limitation, discomfort and pain that become part of our physical signature. Think of the dowager's hump many elderly people develop, and unfortunately, some younger people also acquire. It's so unnecessary. The outer is a direct reflection of the inner and vice versa. Letting your spine have its natural length, and keeping your head up literally changes your view of the world as well as how the world views you. It helps put more self-affirming thoughts in your head. Those thoughts don't stay local. They have powerful energy—energy that resonates within you and without you, which we will discuss next.

13 RESONATE WITH YOUR INTENTIONS

You're about to become an expert in basic vocal rehab, for a moment. Many of the techniques we voice therapists use are meant to boost the energy transfer of what you're putting out, without damaging your vocal cords. When people learn to use their voices efficiently, it helps to avoid potential trauma to the vocal cords, in speaking and singing. That's resonance, and it's what gives our voices their unique qualities. We can distinguish one another from the sound of our voices because of our individual resonance characteristics, the same way we recognize others from their postures and movement patterns. Here's a crash course in voice science: when we talk, our vocal cords vibrate and produce a complex set of frequencies that travel through the throat and mouth and nasal cavity. That's the resonator. Because of the specific size, shape and thickness of our individual resonators, certain frequencies are enhanced, and others are inhibited. That's how we always sound like ourselves.

Voice resonance is a powerful metaphor for how you can live your life, and what you can manifest in your life, once you understand how it works. That is, small vibrations getting turned into much larger vibrations, that radiate outward, with dynamic results. Think of your favorite singers. They can make some big sounds with relatively small instruments. Well, YOU are an instrument, and your vocal instrument sends out your thoughts as well as your sounds. Thoughts and feelings don't just dissolve and vanish, they resonate in an energy field.

Some teachers call this energy field 'The Universe.' You may have heard others call it 'the Ether,' 'the Matrix,' the cosmos, or what have you. Your voice resonates and creates a unique identity. Your emotional and thought patterns come through that energy field too, and influence your life. The thoughts and words you produce, create your experience, especially those about yourself. This is not a new concept.

116

People have been saying it for centuries, and science has caught up and is busy validating it.

Using modern imaging and measurement technology, neuroscientists can watch our brains think. The frequencies of our thoughts can be recorded and measured. When something has a frequency, that means it's vibrating at a certain number of times per second. Particles are moving through a medium – maybe air, maybe space, maybe the Universe. Through your voice, your thoughts travel out of you as vibrations, with a frequency. When doctors or researchers do an EEG (electroencephalogram), the electrodes can't be placed *into* the brain, so they are placed on the skull. Thought energy is emitted outward, and through the resonator. (If this seems "New Agey" to you, be smart and open enough to follow me down this path for a moment.)

Think of it this way: if air and space were stagnant, flights would never be bumpy. But there's movement during air travel: the plane flies through drafts and currents, and that's energy. Consider that your thoughts also move through an energy field— one in which you participate. The thoughts and feeling energy that come out of you enter a resonating space that doesn't judge or discriminate. It takes what it's given. This "soft science" has met "hard science" over the last few decades and is beginning to be well understood. [Read Lynne McTaggert's *The Field,* for a fascinating discussion of this concept that is outgrowing mysticism.]

All resonators work the same way, they transfer energy. Whatever you might call the resonator of your thoughts and words, it works the same as the one inside your body that resonates your voice, but with one important difference. Your voice is unique because you are unique. You can change the size, shape and tension of your throat and mouth to change the sound that comes out—celebrity impersonators prove this all the time. But how your thoughts and feelings resonate is not under your control. You can only control what you put in. When you take that control, you can bring into your life more of the things and people and circumstances you desire.

The frequencies we resonate the most often become the strongest ones, and are going to be further strengthened—no matter what they are. Since a resonator can only broadcast what enters it, be mindful not to send out thoughts and words you don't want as your life experience. What you focus your attention and energy on becomes stronger. Beware: frequent thoughts of lack, blame or resentment, for example, will be reinforced. Focusing on things that you don't like—thoughts of anger, self-pity, jealousy, or other complaints, the Universe is going to make sure that's what you get more of, as you request.

What would you like to receive more of? Writer Baird T. Spalding quotes an Eastern 19th century spiritual master: "Every thought or word we think or speak, be it good or bad, returns to us as certainly as we send it forth." It behooves us to *think* before we think.

The expression "What goes around comes around" springs from real experience. At our most basic level, we're all energy. All life is energy, and is in vibration—moving, expanding and contracting. Vibration travels in waves from its source. The energy of that vibration reflects off whatever it meets, *and* travels back to its source. That's physics, and that's personal. The process of identifying the effects of a damaging childhood and leaving it behind begs the questions: what do you want to carry, what do you want to transmit, and how do you want to affect you and others? The energy you radiate reflects off whatever it contacts, and can also penetrate and affect it.

If you read Masaru Emoto's book *The Hidden Messages in Water*, you'll learn how energy can have a significant effect on water, even energy in a written word or phrase. That was the goal of the experiments that led to Emoto's book and a documentary film of the same name. Part of the experiments involved taping words or phrases, expressions like "Love" or "I hate you" on jars of water—various positive and negative contrasts. In the experiment, the next day the water in the jars was frozen and the crystals examined under a microscope. The researchers saw huge differences. The water in the jars with negative messages showed ice crystals that were gnarled and sickly. The positive messages produced elegant, symmetrical crystalline shapes. Emoto received criticism from the scientific community over his research methods, but his experiments provide startling insights.

What are we humans? 50-60% water! The earth we live on? Nearly three-fourths water. The air we move through and breathe all day? It's full of water vapor. (We call it humidity.) Water is a powerful energy conductor. If you want proof, touch the leads of a 9-volt battery with your finger; you don't feel a thing. Then touch it with your tongue that's coated with watery saliva. Zap! We're all affected by each other's energies. Growing up in dysfunctional families, we can be highly sensitive to someone's negative energy. You know when someone is in a bad mood without him or her saying a word. You can feel it in your gut when someone is angry, upset or irritable, and it's distressing—maybe because it's so familiar. Thoughts and feelings are that powerful.

What you think about yourself and the circumstances of your life sends out more significant energy than you realize. Pessimism, unhappiness, being defensive, or thinking of yourself as not as important as someone else begets more of the same. People who are easily angered and offended get more anger and offense. If you're full of self-effacing thoughts and feelings, and that's all people sense, the results are obvious. Shifting toward positive, self-respecting thoughts will change the trajectory of your life.

This is basis of The Law of Attraction—you've heard of it. It has received a lot of attention in movies like *The Secret, What the Bleep Do We Know*, and more. An entire self-help industry has been built around it. This "law" basically states that what we think about the most is what will show up *in* our lives and *as* our lives. The "resonator" picks up the strongest frequencies we transmit, and intensifies them. It doesn't matter if it's what we want or don't want.

What we call muscle memory is the result of repeated practice. That's also true with our thoughts. Thoreau said, "To make a deep mental path, we must think over and over the kind of thoughts we wish to have dominate our lives." We all do this, mostly unconsciously. Therefore, any constant negative or pessimistic thinking is going to become self-fulfilling. If you grew up in a self-esteem-destroying environment, you carried away damaging, terrible thinking habits. Once they've set up shop in your head, they shape your life. You're worthy of much better, and you can create it. Exceptional begets exceptional. Insert some thoughts of self-respect, capability and appreciation.

In his writing and lectures, the late Dr. Wayne Dyer had a slightly different take on the Law of Attraction: we don't necessarily attract what we want or don't want, we attract what we are. Sooo... who do you want to be? Whatever your answer is, start by acting as that person now in whatever ways you can. Don't doubt your ability. You can become who you want to be, even if you face challenges or meet any resistance. And expect to get various responses from people whenever you start making changes in your behavior and attitudes.

We train people how to treat us. Most people prefer us to stay the way they see us, and some may resist changes we make in our attitudes, behaviors and directions. Behaviors in our families came to be anticipated and demanded. We developed certain patterns, becoming predictable—everyone knew what to expect from us, and we learned to play our roles. Family members expected us to fall in line. When crises arose, the defense mechanisms and coping strategies automatically kicked in. Any change in pattern could make things worse. If we didn't stay in our place and play our expected roles, when things "hit the fan," trouble could spiral out of control. The frustrating reality is that even when we did play our roles, it usually didn't help or prevent anything.

Now that we're adults, our trained childhood patterns can be recognized, and replaced with healthier alternatives that serve us better. One pattern is the tendency to find "our place" in our relationships. It's not a place we necessarily like or consciously choose, it's just automatic. Once the people around us get used to how we have let them treat us, a change will make one of two things happen: either they'll be angry that we're not giving them what they expect, or they'll welcome our growth and support it. When we stray from "our place," it can make some people uncomfortable. We may get called out or punished in some way for threatening the status quo. Please remember, anyone who wants you to be what they want—and not who you are—is not a friend.

Some people don't want others to change if it might mean they'll have to change, too. I've seen this reality at times when doing inpatient consults in the hospital. I've met morbidly obese patients, for example – sometimes 400 pounds or more – who are suffering from medical problems stemming from being that size. They're often unable to work, they have chronic pain and can't move well, they rarely leave the house, they can become clinically depressed. And my heart goes out to them, because when I walk into their room and talk to them, they're usually very nice, delightful people. When I would ask my colleagues, "How could this have happened to them? It takes a lot of

121

groceries to get that big and stay that big." Sometimes it's because someone is feeding them. The person lying in the hospital bed isn't always the only patient. When people get used to our being the way we are, they come to expect it and reinforce it; but if they're the right people for our lives, they'll adjust to changes we make and support us, and reap the benefits with us.

Meaningful change takes courage, determination and adaptability—from us and the people close to us. During my twenties and thirties, my glass was always half empty. I used to joke with my friends and coworkers all the time that everything in my life "takes too long, costs too much and is a general pain in the ass." That was my line. I said it nearly every day. It was no joke, though, it was what I'd created—things took too long, cost too much and even simple, everyday tasks became unnecessary ordeals. Changing my thinking took time and effort, but the result was worth it. Now it's your turn.

If you've lacked self-esteem and self-confidence, you might know where it came from. But now it's all you. You can make things better. Your own process doesn't have to take as long or be as stop-and-start as mine. You *can* change your thoughts and where you put your energy. It's as simple as, change the vibration, change the result. (That's basic voice therapy, in my professional world. Changing the physiology from within changes the acoustics, which changes the perception, and equals a clearer, stronger voice.) And a more fulfilling life experience begins with what you modify and then send out from within.

You can't change your history. But you can start a new history. There is a lot of healing energy in the new awareness of where your life really originated—call it a Higher Intelligence, God, the Creator, Source Energy, First Cause, whatever you're comfortable saying. It's commonly heard in church sermons, that God put you and me here so that He could be here. That means us – no mistake or accident. That's something to be grateful for. It's also a great reminder to get into a vibrational mode that will serve you, by resonating that healthier energy. Let the words of James Twyman, in *The Moses Code,* confirm it for you: "Every thought is a prayer that creates a magnetic attraction, pulling whatever we're thinking about into our lives." Would it be easier if you knew that you aren't alone in this? You have me and this book, and fellow readers, and the God within you. Let that energy resonate, and what comes back to you will be amazing.

Have you ever been told that you're a hard person to compliment? Were you brought up in a hurtful environment? Learning to say thank you graciously if someone says something nice to you, that takes practice. It's not easy to accept credit for a job well done, if you didn't get much credit when your mentality and personality were developing. Then, your goal was to get through a day without feeling humiliated, disregarded, or harshly criticized, or maybe you were tasked with refereeing between family members.

Dysfunctional families aren't based on the kids' accomplishments and successes as students, athletes, artists, or lemonade stand entrepreneurs. Skewed families revolve around the adults, about how the kids are a burden, what parents "sacrificed for the children." A solid but appalling example is the movie *I, Tonya* about Tonya Harding. Some of us have similar experience, not allowed to feel important or valued as kids. Maybe you had a sibling who was favored over you, and you were treated like an unwelcome also-ran who never measured up. The consequences are similar, even if the details differ for our individual stories. Do you feel guilty when you stick up for yourself? Do you accommodate others' wants, and make your own needs less important? Do you let people take advantage of you? Do you feel cruelly judged for being yourself?

If you were overlaid with the mindset of "I don't matter as much," you're going to attract people into your life who are not good for you. Being "fun to pick on" is a logical next step after "hard to compliment." Being praised can inspire a response to downplay the compliment or bat the praise away—in essence, telling the praiser that they're wrong about you. That's not humility, it's a self-negating slam. "Fun to pick on" is because we're inviting it.

125

If you were observing from a distance, you would ask a legitimate question: how can you grow to be a confident, valued individual popular among your peers, who naturally commands respect, if you weren't valued at home first? Some kids become withdrawn and become outcasts at school, and get picked on. Others, depending on their size or temperament, become bullies. It's not uncommon, especially during our school years. But any respect that bullies "command" is artificial. Kids who bully aren't necessarily bad kids; they might just be copying what they see or receive at home. They could be getting bullied themselves or watching other people in the house getting bullied. Or they might be expressing bottled-up aggression against someone who can't retaliate. Sadly, bullying is at a new level in our digital age. With social media, modern-day bullies have more at their disposal to target and hurt others. It seems harder today to be a kid from a dysfunctional family than it was when I was growing up. The consequences of being different can be more public. As adults, bullies come in several varieties: physical bullies, social bullies, intellectual bullies as suggested in chapter 10, and workplace bullies. We've all likely run into bullies at times, but we don't have to be targets and get picked on – if we shift our way of thinking about ourselves.

You can change self-defeating or ineffectual ways of thinking. You can even alter programming that's been in place for years. Bemoaning the past won't change the past, but you don't need to. You can change your Right Now. **Right Now is yours to create**. No matter what happened in the past—twenty or thirty years ago, or even a couple of hours ago—you're living your life Here and Now. Now is when you can be vibrantly present. You're here Now. God is here Now. Harness the energy of Right Now, and move beyond any limits of the past. Showing up and making every Now count takes intention and focus. Many of the habits we developed in painful, tormenting early environments may limit us as adults, relative to our self-concept, but nothing is permanent unless we allow it to be.

Nothing is un-changeable, nothing is un-improvable.

"Wait a second! I don't dislike myself. I'm not some second-rate person. I'm not unworthy." That's right, you're not. Neither am I. But the subconscious mind has other ideas, when you've had an "other than normal" upbringing. Think about how you've treated yourself so far in your life, what you've allowed yourself to have, to earn, to enjoy, and the goals you've pursued. Do you give yourself credit? Do you feel worthy of rewards for your accomplishments? You're probably worth more than you've allowed yourself to be. Have you held yourself back, because your subconscious mind—that part you're not aware of—was trained that you don't deserve to be happy and prosperous and achieve lofty goals? Your subconscious whispers that you're not as capable or as important as others; when you accomplish something consequential, it gets unsettled and tries to drag you back down where it insists you belong. Since it's easier to see truths through others' experience, see if an example of mine brings up any similar memories of your own.

I studied martial arts for eleven years, and it probably saved my life when I was a teenager. Not because I got into fights—I didn't. The study and practice gave me three important things: it helped me through a critical period by providing a physical outlet for nervous energy; it surrounded me with positive influences, and introduced me to Eastern philosophy. I was awarded my First-Degree black belt when I was 19, and it was a surprise. Sensei walked up to me before class one evening, took off the belt he'd been wearing for years and tied it around my waist. This is an honor in the karate world, and I was humbled and grateful; but it meant I'd have to wear that belt every day as part of my uniform for my fellow students to see. Some of them had been studying longer than I had, but hadn't been promoted with the same speed and success. I worried what they would think. I'd worked hard, practiced for hours every day and sweated gallons. I studied with passion, and immersed myself in the philosophy of ancient martial arts as physical art forms and as a way of life: peace and humility, nothing like the brutality seen in MMA fights. I passed all my promotion tests along the way and earned my black belt in about four years. But on receiving my black belt, my subconscious mind reared up and barked, "How dare you! You don't deserve that. You're inferior!" I practically snuck away hoping no one would notice me, worried that my fellow students would think I was trying to be someone I was not, criticizing or judging me. I got mad at them for the thoughts and opinions I was assigning to them. It was an unhealthy internal mind game that I'd played far too frequently.

Eleanor Roosevelt famously said, "No one can make me feel inferior without my permission." My subconscious mind wasn't as evolved as hers. Is that a feeling you share, like you're on a different maturation schedule? Know that no matter how late it feels, you *can* bloom, and you deserve to let yourself do it. There's no such thing as "too late." Growing up in a dysfunctional family can make you a late bloomer, because your experience was so very different from some other children's. It's common to compare ourselves to others, but when we do, we can become discouraged or resentful; we see others of the same age enjoying the kind of life that we think we should have. Looking back with sorrow or fury, ruminating about what might have been or "what should have been" isn't just unproductive, it's self-punishing.

Be encouraged, even excited, to look ahead to see what you can be and what you can create. The instruction to "Play where the puck is going to be" also means to appreciate what is Now, where things actually happen. You can create the future you desire when you give your best to every Right Now opportunity you get. The journey is supposed be as much fun and as big a reward as the eventual destination. What that means, is "Don't just plan, do!" Have goals, but live your life, too – Now. Right Now is where you can intentionally create a future that can unfold in unexpectedly wonderful ways. Again, look at the point through another's experience.

I was taking high school-level math classes in my late 30s, and to say I wasn't thrilled about that would be an understatement. Why was I in those classes? I'd probably had the intellectual ability to handle algebra when everyone else did (or maybe it wasn't a lack of intellect but the emotional damage from being consumed by the upheaval at home.) I'd been able to work around my lack of advanced math skill, until I applied for PhD programs. Every grad school applicant has to take the GRE exam (which has absolutely nothing to do with life as we know it, we just have to take it.) I'd been accepted and did well in a Master's program at a leading university—until I hit the wall. So there I was, 38 years old, some two decades older than most of my classmates, attending a community college at night to learn algebra—three straight semesters, with plans to retake the GRE and hopefully hoist my math scores. A late Bloomer indeed, but I learned; and it ended up having tremendous value for my professional *and* personal life. I showed up for Now and created something, meeting people who appreciated my drive and ambition, who befriended me and helped me pursue my career goals in ways I didn't know I could. This is the reward for showing up for Now and giving it your best, in any small way.

Now that you know the future is determined by what you do with your Now, it's still important to have guidance. There are multiple principles, ideas and practices to learn and be inspired by and put to deliberate use. That knowledge and inspiration might take time to find if you've spent years playing catch up, but if you begin where you are Right Now, you're right on schedule. This book could be your beginning. Reading about other people's experiences and growth processes can expand your understanding of yourself. The teachings of philosophers, spiritual leaders and mind-body practitioners are all available for you. Begin! You're worth it. Being a late bloomer is no big deal. Plenty of people begin again, at all stages of life. One of my past personal self-judging sayings was that "All my personal accomplishments happened ten years too late." (That's the kind of bullshit that gets in your head when your self-esteem bottoms out. You don't have to go there. I already did it for you. You're welcome.)

When you allow yourself to be exactly who you are and begin becoming who you want to be, everything is just as it should be, and will fall into place. You don't need to compare yourself to anybody else's developmental "schedule." That's bogus anyhow. Your point is to bloom, to blossom. Now. It's your time—even if you're 38 years old in a class of 18-year-old Algebra I students. You're never too old to bloom, and to direct your life the way you choose to, to pursue and achieve the goals that satisfy you, to be who you were created to be. Right Now is yours, to appreciate, to give your best to and to craft to your liking.

How do you picture a "normal" person? Do you consider yourself normal? Ever think you might be fundamentally flawed? Ever had someone bluntly tell you "how not normal you are," because they think you should be something other than who you are—you're wrong because you're not what they think you should be? It hurts to hear; but when you wanted their approval, did you bend and twist yourself to conform to their expectations, trying to be what someone thought you should be? It's exhausting, and that's no way to treat yourself. It's past the time for you to put a new spin on "normal" and take a new perspective. "Weird" is the label I sometimes received, when I didn't conform to others' expectations while I was growing up. What about you? It's time to reframe that label, too.

"Normal" and "weird" aren't defined like they used to be. Look around. The standard shifts all the time. Who and what is "normal" or "weird" is dramatically changed from society's previous standards. Some people get idolized for how "other than normal" they are—often they become celebrities, and they're considered exotic.

It's time you found out what many centered, elite vocalists already know: you are not "normal," you've never been normal, and "normal" isn't a goal to try for. "Normal" people don't stand out—exceptional people do. "Normal" isn't particularly persuasive or inspiring. You need to be exceptional! You can aspire to be much more than just like the crowd.

When my colleagues and I speak to music professionals, choral groups, and especially to pop and rock stars—or wannabes—we remind singers that they are unique among musicians. Vocalists don't put their instruments back into a case and walk away when they're done using them. They carry their instruments inside them all day and use them for other purposes besides singing. That's why those instruments demand exquisite care. The person *is* the instrument. Vocalists can't treat themselves as separate from what makes them unique, the way they imagine "normal" people can.

People are different from each other for good reasons. In his book, *Thoughts on Man*, Konosuke Matsushita, the founder of Panasonic, states, "Variety makes life more interesting and it ensures that there is always something to make up for whatever is lacking." Read that again. He doesn't know you personally, but he wrote this insight for you. You have a unique contribution to make. You can thrive in your "other than normal-ness," and other people might also benefit from your being "other than normal." We all need to integrate reasonably into our communities, to get along, and to work together for the common good and our own benefit; we're not just zombies without the ability to make choices, who act alike and pursue the same things. That's worse than stagnant, that's boring and counter-productive! (Imagine a world where every woman wanted to pair with Jon Hamm, or every man wanted Beyonce. In that world that'd be "normal" but impossible!) Consider admitting that we could be "weird" in others' eyes, and still be just fine.

Dysfunctional families don't produce "normal people," but that's not automatically a bad thing. Picasso didn't see the world in "normal" ways. The Beatles, Stravinsky and even Beethoven translated feelings into sounds never heard before. Would you blame them for not being "normal?" We can turn "weird" into exceptional. You're already halfway there.

Think back to your school days. Did some kids call you weird or treat you that way? Did you fit in with your peers? How about now? Do you feel accepted and comfortable in your social settings or in an extended family? Do you attract the kind of people into your life that you want, who like and respect you and bring out your best? Do you often feel more tolerated than

133

respected? Do you fit in well with the people at your job?

If you've felt like you've had a hard time fitting in well, consider whether you have been effectively taught how to fit in. The feelings and flavor of your childhood shaped you two specific sources: 1) your self-respect and self-confidence, and general sense of belonging; and 2) the social skills your parents were supposed to model for you, and what they told you about yourself. What messages did you receive when you were growing up? See if this experience sounds familiar.

When I was in fifth grade, my mom put me in the car after school one afternoon and drove us to an office. She introduced me to a man I'd never seen before, and left us together. I didn't know who he was or what was going on. Turns out, he was a counselor. He sat me down and began with, "Your mom says you're not happy," and he proceeded to ask how could he help me. And on we went. I spent over an hour feeling blindsided, invaded and uncomfortable, trying to convince us both that I was a normal kid. It worked, because I never had to go back. Maybe it helped my mom feel like she did her due diligence, without having to look at what was really going on. Those pre-teen and teenage years were confusing. Despite the chaos in our house— the terrifying brawls, the embarrassing public scenes, the drinking, the screaming, and being told often that I was the one with the problem, that I was the one who needed help. Maybe that counselor, speaking to my mom privately afterwards, knew what I'm about to tell you.

Being an unhappy kid or labeled as a "weird" kid is a lot like having asthma. It's not an isolated condition, it's a symptom of an underlying problem. What happens when you have asthma? You're usually prescribed medications supposed to control the condition, given a rescue inhaler and directed to use it when needed. These treat the symptoms and keep asthma more manageable, but that's all it does – keeps it manageable. You still have asthma. If the underlying cause doesn't get addressed, attacks can recur. You keep that rescue inhaler handy. How is this relatable? Some voice therapy patients have serious asthma, and damage their vocal cords with frequent intense coughing. They get professional guidance to control their coughing and re-train their breathing patterns to support their overall wellness.

What if the household you grew up in was toxic? What if you were often at the effect of neurotic adults' self-indulgent behaviors, or had their damage inflicted on you? What if you were forced prematurely into adult responsibilities?

What's the asthma inhaler for that?!?

Being a weird or unhappy kid cannot be treated or counseled out of you while the problem that created it continues – a problem you can't control. Of course, counseling later can help, when you're older and have the ability to take in the healing you want and need. But when you're a kid, you don't have the understanding or the power to remedy the situation that makes you feel like an outsider, standing out in an odd way from other kids.

Your social competence and success begin in childhood, at home. We're supposed to gain self-confidence and a sense of being equal to others, if we grow up "normally." But when our people skills and personal style develop in a distorted environment, we grow different, and usually not in a good way in others' eyes. That's tough for a kid. Developmental psychologist Erik Erikson describes a period of our childhood when we're ideally supposed to become confident with who we are and learn to see ourselves as competent. We each had different experiences, and took our "other than normal-ness" to school with us every day, and maybe got a "weird" label that wasn't even deserved—other kids viewed us through their own "weirdness," which skewed their visions of us.

There are emotional, and physical, risks to being a "weird" kid. See if some of these common results resonate in your life.

- Being ostracized by many of your peers, or getting in trouble or fights because others take advantage of your feelings of insecurity.
- Being used by people because you don't know other ways to get their approval.
- Letting yourself be treated badly, accepting and even helping others treat you badly, imagining people can't put you down if you beat them to it.
- Acting out by becoming a bully yourself. This is how some kids compensate for what they're going through in their own families. Maybe they were selfish or evil, but possibly their home life could have been twice as challenging as yours.
- The saddest consequence could be taking it out on yourself. People who are "cutters," with multiple ER visits and scarred forearms, often have families that might explain some reasons for the razor blades. Some people overeat and purposely become obese to shield themselves from the struggles of relationships, because of an absence of self-esteem. When you read their stories, do it with sympathy and understanding.

When your social and emotional development is amiss, or if self-esteem is like a foreign language to you, your group of childhood friends won't likely be the same as for other kids your age—weird attracts weird. You may have been expected to behave at home like an adult—the only "adult" in your house?— because the actual adults were too self-absorbed, mired in their dramas and unadmitted damage.

Need a graphic example? When I was 14, I came home from school one afternoon to see several spectators gathered across the street from my house, with two police cars and an ambulance out front. I joined the audience of eight or nine neighbors, as EMTs wheeled out my screaming, hysterical mom, strapped onto a stretcher. We listened to them debate which psychiatric hospital they should take her to. Then, police officers escorted my stepfather out in handcuffs. The neighbors weren't shocked, they were well trained by then – it wasn't unusual for cops to be at our house. That afternoon, Mom had called the police saying that her husband poisoned her. That wasn't true, we discovered later. They were just shit-faced and having a fight. When the police officers arrived, my stepfather got physical and tried to push them out of the house. He spent the night sleeping it off in a holding cell, while mom spent a few days drying out in the hospital.

Everyone has a story, some more shocking than others. In a support group, one young woman shared that while she was growing up, she would ride the bus around town by herself— paying bills, doing grocery shopping and taking care of other family business—when she was in the second grade!! How can a kid who plays that role in the family be "normal?"

You may already know, there are alternatives to becoming a pseudo-adult when you're the kid in a crazy, unstable environment. Kids from troubled homes often act out or behave badly; there's plenty of published research about it. It's described as a defense mechanism—the "You're so bad that I'll be worse" theory. It's as if a kid's subconscious mind says, "My family *can't* be this weird and a laughingstock. *I'll* be the problem. My family is fine." Also, some kids can become more accident-prone or sickly, and demand attention because it's the only way they know to feel cared about and loved. My sister played that dual role in her own way for years, drawing negative attention toward herself and taking it away from the family, but not always successfully and not consciously. She got injured and had other medical problems—not her fault, just higher maintenance and more demanding of attention. Later, as a teenager, she got involved with the "partying" crowd and was arrested once, having been under someone's bad influence, and didn't have a good reputation at school.

It can take a lot of effort to fit in with the kids in your grade at school, when your social development is "normal." To a kid burdened by family issues, it's an even bigger struggle to relate well to your peers. There's a compatibility mismatch, with little in common besides just going to the same school. As an example, when I was a teenager most of my friends were either quite a bit older or a lot younger than me—it was easier to relate to responsible adults than to fun-loving teens (since I had to become an "adult" in some ways before I was a teenager,) but since I was maturing slower socially and emotionally than kids my chronological age, it was easy for me to bond with people who were younger. So where could I belong, and with whom? Where would I fit in? I know now these are common feelings. Our challenge is to channel negative experiences properly, and not pass along bullying as an adult. We've all seen intellectual bullies and workplace bullies. Don't be that guy!

If your peer group looks different from you, this can be a simple explanation: you're at a different social-emotional level. This isn't just a grade school phenomenon. When I was 25, I was briefly romantically involved with a high school senior. A bad idea, and lopsided—she just used me to buy beer for her and her friends. The human need to fit in somewhere is powerful. We can be so open to influence from the need for approval that it's easy to fall in with whoever gives us acceptance and self-esteem. That's when misplaced trust becomes a problem.

Academic literature tells us that because children from dysfunctional families learn not to trust their parents, they can end up developing a general suspicion of most people. And while that can be true for many, so is the opposite—that we are *aching* to trust, which leads to taking big emotional risks. We can be very accepting and forthright people, desperately looking

138

for a bond we feel has been missing. Does this explain why, if you've ever given someone your trust or loyalty, only to painfully discover that they were playing you? It's not that uncommon for children with damaged trust to be taken advantage of, or manipulated, or even to deny clear reality, as long as there's some feeling of acceptance and belonging.

People with damaged trust "issues" can attract people whose issues are equal to or worse than ours. It's true that like attracts like, but it also can attract worse, like narcissists or even sociopaths. We don't need a pile of research studies to know that a dysfunctional upbringing won't help us in later life, when we're hoping to make friends or attract romantic partners who are right for us. If you've had stabs in the heart, know that you can expect better, and create better—because you're not weird, you're exceptional.

Your experience makes you different. Acknowledge it. In fact, celebrate it. Recognize that you're not ordinary, you're exceptional! It might take time to come to terms with being unconventional and different—remember Cyndi Lauper before she was "Cyndi Lauper." Can you consider that your situation is a positive? If you have an "other-than-normal" history, a life differently lived, maybe the average person might think of you as "weird." Great! Please consider that **most "average" and "normal" people lack qualities that your life experience may have granted you in abundance: ingenuity, creativity, resilience, the ability to think on your feet, to negotiate and not lose your cool in a tense situation.** Some individuals empathize well and enter helping professions (remember "the wounded healer?") and have positive impacts on others' lives. Your life experience has given you empathy and valuable skills.

"Weird" gets things done! The profound, world-transforming discoveries, achievements and teachings throughout history haven't come from "average" or "normal" people. Exceptional people change the world; they upset the norm. Oddballs, heretics, lawbreakers, and anarchists change the world. Socrates was weird. Sojourner Truth was weird. Mozart was weird. Galileo was weird. Mother Theresa was weird. Gandhi was weird. Jesus was weird. The entire world has benefited from how "weird" these people were. You come from the same Source, with all the same attributes of your Creator. Today, look at who is granted Nobel Prizes in the sciences and humanities. "Normal" people? Modern tech sector giants like Bill Gates and Meg Whitman were geeks when they were school-age kids; despite the criticism they've received, they have changed the world. Need more validation? Nutrition author Douglas Graham reminds us, "Every single advancement on the planet was made by a nonconformist."

Talk to any surgeon and he or she will tell you that when we're cut open, we're all basically the same. Realize who you really are, a God particle, a Divinely created being, of The Creator, who fashioned creative beings—including You. Sensory awareness educator Charlotte Selver said, "Realize that every breath in you and every drop of blood in you is the same life substance as in everybody else, and it's just as important and precious as that of everybody else." Changing your inner world leads to change in your outer experience, for you and the lives you touch, just like all the people who have changed the world at large for the better. They did what they did while being called weird, and much worse.

Our brains and our psyches work a lot like our muscles. They adapt and grow and become stronger, if we engage them and ask it of them. You can shape and mold yourself as you wish, knowing that God and His Unlimited Universe has your back. Are you weird? Nice! Enjoy it. Forget about "fitting in." Blaze your own trail and enjoy who you are without apology—no apologies for things you didn't do, no apologizing for your very presence, no apologizing for apologizing! You can become the

"Exceptional" you're meant to be, deliberately. It's not as hard as you've thought. Keep reading.

16 THERE'S A BETTER WAY TO DO THIS

Back in college I took a class called "Courtship & Marriage," because I thought it would be helpful with my relationship at the time. The title was misleading. Nothing about courtship, the class was about how to effectively raise and manage a family. We were taught that the home environment should be nurturing and supportive, because such a setting is vital to children's physical and social development. That class oddly never mentioned a dysfunctional family.

I spent the entire semester stunned. The lectures and assigned reading about how a good, healthy family should operate made me laugh out loud. Whether they were talking about the ideal family or what a "normal" family was supposed to be, it certainly didn't match *my* experience. My childhood home was just an address. I sat through every class with the same thoughts: "What family is like this? These folks don't have a clue!" I threw my textbooks in the dumpster at the end of the semester. I didn't want that naïve bullshit passed on to the next poor dupe. My childhood reality was so drastically NOT like the "normal," healthy, family described, just hearing about it left me astonished and pissed off.

So, how do we reconcile that discrepancy? First, forget about "normal." In this context, it's subjective. Focus your energy on acting to love yourself, and developing an appropriate love of others. You are here on purpose, like everyone else. It sounds simple, but it's challenging. It takes work. You don't just light incense, sit cross-legged on the floor and chant "Loooove," and suddenly life is beautiful. Go back to the ideas offered so far, and read on for more. Use them, practice them, and watch the experiences they create start shifting your attitude. Use them as blueprints, to help you begin treating yourself with the love you totally deserve. When that kind of energy is coming out of you, watch the amazing things that can happen.

If the idea of self-love isn't comfortable yet, then think of it as acceptance of exactly who you are. You are worthy, and you've paid your dues. Honor the life you have created, and what you can create with it. Take an objective look, and appreciate all the tools you have to work with, as you form experiences that you create with gratitude, love and forgiveness. Don't crush your potential by looking backwards with judgment, blame, or justification for anything you're not. Growing up in a toxic environment isn't a "get out of jail free" excuse card, but it doesn't have to be a noose around your neck. Understanding the effects of your personal history is helpful to your growth process, but there is nothing good gained by exploiting it.

No matter where you've been, or where in your life you are right now, two readily accessible resources are your thoughts and your intention. Don't look to the past to find all the answers; just ask the right questions now: "What and whom do I want to be today?" And if you're a parent, "How would I like my children to remember me?"

Parenting is an enormous, unending task. Not just anybody can do it, and not just anybody should. Parents take on the responsibility of children physically, socially, emotionally, spiritually, financially, and more. Home and family are supposed to be safe havens. Dysfunctional homes are the opposite. **There's no "shelter from the storm" if home *is* the storm.**

Healthy and effective parenting, requires evolving as a parent as the kids get older. Teenagers don't need their noses wiped. They will need you in different ways as they grow and become more independent and self-reliant. Parents must need them differently, too: children grow, change and evolve. If the parents don't, it's a recipe for trouble.

My folks didn't evolve much, as parents or as spouses. My

older sister and I were both adopted, possibly because our mom felt unfulfilled and disillusioned at that point in her life, and maybe dissatisfied with her marriage. She planned to fill the void by bringing babies into the house who would cling to her and worship her. (This is not an uncommon tale.) Becoming a parent wasn't about the kids, it was about her. My mom was a decent, hardworking, kindhearted woman. She had some personal issues—like a lot of people—but didn't have the internal resources to handle those issues. As we got older and became more autonomous, the fulfillment we gave her as dependent babies faded away. What might have been clinical depression gradually set in, and she was lost in booze by the time I was in third or fourth grade.

Dad was initially ambivalent about becoming a parent, my sister and I later learned, but he accepted the role and did the things he thought he should do for us: providing for his family and supporting some of our activities. He never knew his own father, so he didn't have a model to follow. Basically, dad checked out and spent most of his time in the garage where he had his workshop (man cave.) By the time my sister and I were school-age, our parents' marriage had stagnated, and they grew apart. Eventually, their personal and marital problems overran the family. Even when mom worked hard and stayed sober and tried to put her life on a more spiritual course, dad continued drinking. Their lives went in opposite directions, and when I was 13 they separated for a year. Dad answered the doorbell one night, and a process server handed him divorce papers. He soon moved out, and mom hooked up with a man she'd met at AA meetings. My freshman year of high school was a train wreck of constant chaos. She went to Vegas with this guy and married him (without legally divorcing my dad,) and brought the new guy into the house. His sobriety quickly did a 180, and mom followed him. For the next several years, dysfunction climbed to new heights at our house. My sister and I somehow made it through our early teens without Child Protective Services whisking us away. By then, we were old enough to take care of ourselves, but we paid a price. This book is in your hands because my experience is not unique, but the way I learned to reboot my life may serve you on your journey.

If you're a parent now, and you want your kids to experience a different childhood than you had, you don't want to replicate your experience; and it's not enough to just do the opposite. You need to acquire new information and new attitudes—for your children's sake and yours. Some of your own scars can fade. If you're already doing this, and seeing your family thrive, good for you—keep it up. Making a nurturing and supportive haven for your children also serves you and your fellow parent. You're doing good, but be cautious: don't let your ego's needs overshadow the needs of your trusting, vulnerable children. Having children for the right reasons means you want to be a family that grows and evolves together. Your self-fulfillment is *your* job. Families become dysfunctional when the kids are assigned the responsibility of running the household or providing the parents' happiness.

Successful households are not about having gobs of money and giving everyone expensive clothes and gadgets. Some of the most exceptional people came from humble beginnings, even from abject poverty. The values that you model and teach are the most important: love with respect and self-respect, humility, leading by example, accountability, spiritual awareness. Your job is parenting with fairness and consistency.

If you continue to grow and evolve, as a person and as a parent, your kids will hopefully have a reliable and inspiring role model. All parents make mistakes; do your best to make sure your mistakes are one-offs rather than patterns. If you're paying attention and genuinely care, you can learn from your mistakes and improve. I'm a former radio personality and promotion director who had to constantly chase ratings and knows what it's like to be fired; I can personally confirm the adage that your defeats make you better than your victories. If you teach your kids love and forgiveness instead of judgment and blame, all of you are off to a great start. When they get older, they can look back with fondness and gratitude; they won't need to deny or push away their reality to protect their fragile psyches, or lie to anyone about who they are.

What about your kids' mistakes? They'll make plenty of bad decisions. You know from your own childhood, that it's the parents' job to protect and teach the kids, not blame and shame them for their mistakes. Their young minds are still developing. They can't process and consider risks and consequences the way adults do. They won't be able to until they're well into their 20s. You are there to educate them. You want your parenting to be lasting and meaningful, creating a positive relationship, not only meting out discipline when they screw up.

Your kids give you the chance for a different parent-child relationship than the one you had as a child. Be there for them, remember that they're not there for you. It's okay to punish them when they need it, just be sure the correction is in proportion to the mistake. Also, make it soon enough after the mess-up that the child understands why he/she is being punished. If you've been teaching and modeling for them all along, they'll probably know when they've messed up; even though they won't like being punished, it's easier for them to "get it" and they won't despise you for it. When a punishment is delivered with firm kindness and not vengeance, the relationship isn't damaged. Forget any cliché like "Love the sinner, hate the sin." Kids aren't "sinners," they make mistakes and bad decisions. Children need a safe environment in which to learn from their mistakes and failures. You love your kids and you want them to love you back, not be afraid of you or hate you.

Once, after a remote radio broadcast, several kids stayed after

147

to hang out with me. I was umpiring their baseball game and having great fun watching them have great fun. After a while, one boy asked what time it was. Someone shouted out the time, and the poor kid burst into tears and ran off. Apparently, he was supposed to be home earlier, and he knew he was going to be in big trouble. Looking desperate, he rode away in tears on his bike, shouting "Now I'm going to get killed by my *dumb* parents!" I can only hope that he was exaggerating.

We can prove philosopher Will Durant right or wrong. He wrote, "Show me your children and I will tell you what you are." Do you reflect your upbringing, and what do you want your kids to be? Now that you're acquiring more self-awareness, you don't have to blame struggles or failures on anyone else. Radiating hostility or having a chip on your shoulder is not what you want to pass on. As the parent, you lead by example whether you mean to or not. Your kids are watching and absorbing *all* your behavior – the good and the not-so-good. Your childhood was what it was. Acknowledge it, learn from it, and then leave it where it belongs. You have the rest of your life ahead of you, and you have better things to do. Move your life forward, and start Now—don't quit because of past mistakes or failures. Stay determined and press on. When your kids learn that from watching you, you're giving them much better odds of success in whatever they do.

Let me offer you what I finally realized about my own family: "Maybe my parents raised me the best way they could with the tools they had. Maybe it wasn't completely their fault." (On the other hand, maybe it *was* their fault, but keep an open mind here.) Maybe your parents didn't have what you have now. They grew up in a different era, and you don't know the full story of how they were raised, what their childhood experiences were and how they coped with them.

Assuming they had good intentions, they may have passed

along what they had. But your kids don't have to get the same hard lessons. Give them the benefit of your wisdom and experience, so their experiences and beliefs can prepare them for what the world is really like once it's their time to be adults. That's how you pay it forward.

With an iPod, you get to choose how much memory it has. Mine has 32 gigs, enough room for several full-length movies. How many gigs of memory do our brains have? How many "movies" can they hold? We have so much room for storage in our heads. How about your file storage? Every child's mental library is filled with memory movies, many often not feel-good. Your own kids' mental iPods will have a different library from yours. You can create many more uplifting scenes for your child.

You can teach your children to give and receive what you didn't get: sufficient love, self-respect, how to aim high and pursue passions. Those are solid roots. Regardless of your childhood experience, you can teach the next generation and give you and your children what you both need. Enrich both of you at the same time. When you make a mistake, acknowledge and keep teaching—it simply means you have more to learn. You will enjoy your adulthood more by enjoying your kids' childhood, and letting *them* enjoy it.

Bear in mind that what you teach your own children will affect their social circle, too. At some point, your children's peers will have as much or more influence on them, and your kids will influence their friends. When adult supervision in my house was lacking, and much of the adult behavior on display was atrocious, some of the neighborhood kids would come over to do things they could never do at their own houses: smoke pot, drink liquor, have sex in our backyard. Know that your influence on your kids and their friends extends beyond your property line. Although we can't prove cause-and-effect, some of those former neighborhood kids have struggled with serious personal issues as adults.

Please remember that ultimately, we're raised by more than our own parents. We have influential teachers, extended family, our friends' parents, and many others. Some children of dysfunctional households adopt surrogate families, some lasting a lifetime. I was able to enjoy many childhood holidays because other families welcomed me into their celebrations. That's not an indictment of my own relatives—we exchanged gifts on Christmas morning, and it was usually fine. But we were not a close family who enjoyed spending time together. Many Thanksgivings and Christmases were spent at friends' houses, folded into their family celebrations.

In fairness, our hurts, frustrations, confusions, or social missteps don't only stem from a dysfunctional childhood. The attitudes, mentality, and distorted feelings of self-worth we developed at home can steer us into relationships that hurt us even more. We had many influences growing up; our job as self-aware adults is to weed out the negatives.

It's a blessing when you have in your childhood world, people who model other ways of being good adults. Good alternative influences can be extended family, neighbors, clergy, or in my case, karate instructors. Some kids are lucky enough to have good alternative influences around them growing up. The other influences you have around you compete with your home environment. The parents or older siblings of my friends in the neighborhood, would look at me and say, "*You're* okay." I took that to mean, "I don't like your family, but I can handle *you*." I thought it was a disrespectful and hurtful insult. Looking back now, I can see that they might have meant "The problem is not you, kid." A few people were genuinely concerned, having witnessed some of the shouting and shocking behaviors that poured out of my house; they became surrogate families and

150

were good role models. If you had outside positive influences, appreciate them and appreciate what they did for you. If you're a parent now, pay it forward and extend yourself to others' children.

The most important fact to remember is that you're a grown-up now—you have choice and control and can bat away old bad reflexes when they pop up. Now you can be the 'normal' you envied as a child, and give it to your kids and their friends. While it's not your responsibility to parent other people's children, remember that you're being watched. What you demonstrate as a parent, as a good adult, matters very very much. You might even become surrogate family for other kids from challenging homes. If you can provide a positive example, based on what you learned the hard way, you can save them from the feeling of being hit upside the head with a two-by-four if they realize the distance between what they experienced and what's good. Possibly even more important, you'll make lemonade out of lemons: you will transform the pain you experienced into healing for a child.

A dysfunctional homelife is either a constant parade of painful events or the nervous anticipation of them, and that angst rarely leaves you. Collecting baseball cards is a hobby for many kids, but collecting stress is an affliction and a burden. Stress is endless when we don't know how home is going to feel from one day to the next, or even from one hour to the next. Sometimes worse, there are times when we know exactly what we'll walk into. For all we knew, it might have been every family's reality behind closed doors. Let's just focus on one family. In the physiology of chronic stress, without relief, we pay for it— especially as we get older.

To this day, when I hear someone slam a door or raise their voice, I become uncomfortable and nervous for a moment. Developmental years spent with no power over an erratic, randomly changing environment can develop high anticipation of more stress. You have 50-50 odds of taking a life-skill away from your childhood: while the echoes of a small, present moment may spark old reflexes, you might also have learned to be calmer under fire, having lived through something similar before. Given that it's possible to overreact to a relatively minor stress, even the anticipation can trigger an emotional, mental, and physical reaction in your body. Stress is part of modern life, but you want to react to stress that's present and real—not the replay of an old reflex reaction.

You don't need to be told, chronic stress is bad for you. Letting it attack your body without any means of release will eventually cause physical symptoms. In tenth grade, I came to school every day with an uncontrollable eye twitch. People would ask me what was wrong with my eye. I had no answer. It was a strange muscle spasm with a life of its own. My family wasn't able to see any connection between my nervous tic and the life they created at home. As usual, they asked what was wrong with *me*. The twitch gradually stopped when I began studying martial arts, and the stress that had been piling up finally had a "release valve."

Luckily, nature has given us a free antidote: exercise. It's an effective, natural outlet for everyday stress. You deserve a physical activity that you regularly enjoy. You can use your "me time" to keep your nervous system stable, but physically working off stress is powerful, too. Anyone can benefit from regular exercise, but becoming a gym rat sweating on cardio machines or heaving iron isn't the only way. A brisk 30-minute walk—or 15 minutes, or a run—is good, even better if you can do in the open air. The book *Earthing* by Clinton Ober recommends running or walking barefoot on the earth—Not on concrete. Some people enjoy gardening; go cycling or swimming if you're into that, or just grab a ball and shoot some hoops. If you go to a gym, many memberships come with a menu of group exercise classes. If you'd rather, Tai Chi, Qiqong, Hatha Yoga, or dancing are all wonderful stress relievers. Studies published in the New England Journal of Medicine showed that frequent dancing also reduces the risk of dementia, so if dancing is something you enjoy, go ahead and get your groove on. If you're a musician, strap on a guitar, or sit at the drum kit and make some noise. Just do something physical.

Dysfunctional families leave lasting psychological and emotional scars; they distort your thinking, and the long-term neurochemical imbalances in your body can also create physiological consequences. Do you already feel what constant high stress can do to you over time? Do you take medication for hypertension? Do you have lupus or other autoimmune disease? Some medical diagnoses are more than just bad luck, unhealthy ancestors, or the results of an unhealthy diet. The results of frequent chaos, conflict, torment, anxiety, crises, disappointments, or anger ramped up your nervous system. That put you in a constant fight-or-flight state. If both current events and flashbacks do it now, you need physical activity to discharge the nervous energy.

As a vocologist, much of my clinical caseload is patients in chronic states of stress. They come in with tight, aching necks and shoulders, unhealthy breathing patterns, and voices that require way too much effort for unsatisfactory results. They—and sometimes the doctors who referred them—can't find why. Chronic stress can go unrecognized for a long time and then manifest all at once, in a diagnosis or even a 9-1-1 call. One somatic discipline (Associative Awareness Technique®) often has the effect of helping the patient release their locked-in fight-or-flight muscular tension: at times, people lying on my table have practically started convulsing, discharging nervous tension that has been trapped in their body for years.

When stress hormones race through your system too much and too often, it's only a matter of time before they wreak havoc. When you're stressed and on guard all the time, something will eventually give way. Your body isn't designed to keep energy stuck and immobile. That hyperarousal keeps muscles constantly tensed, and can lead to frequent headaches or chronic pain. The immune system especially takes a hit, putting you at risk for illness or even degenerative diseases. Have you noticed, you can be more susceptible to getting a cold when stressed out? (A good example is finals week at school.) That same reality affects the longer-term health risks of chronic stress and repeated traumatic experiences. (If you'd like a greater understanding of the effects of chronic stress, read Dr. Robert Scaer's book *The Body Bears the Burden*. It does, the book explains how.)

It's time to remember that you're a person, too. If you were trained to deal with your family's problems by serving the needs of others, you were trained that their needs are "more important" than yours. It served everyone in the household for you to forget that you're an individual too, with your own identity, and your own needs. Throughout my teens and early 20s, I would leave the house and be ME somewhere else all day. When I got home, I'd morph into the family's therapist, life coach, sparring partner, marriage counselor, co-dependent, or the peacekeeper. No doubt, you have your own list of roles. "Normal" parent-child boundaries don't exist in a dysfunctional family, and that reality delivers a lot of nervous tension. If that tension doesn't have a reasonable release, it turns into something else—for me it was a nervous tic. Some people can even develop a reaction where accumulated stress "converts" into a physical disorder; examples of debilitating conversion reactions include paralyzed or numb limbs, or a lost voice. I see this frequently as a vocal therapist—someone's unrelenting stress moves into their larynx, and their voice becomes a tiny whisper (despite having normal anatomy and normal reflex functions like coughing and yawning.) Not having a "voice" is both a reality and a metaphor for children in dysfunctional families. Do you suppose I got into radio to talk for a living, to make up for all the lost years when I couldn't have a voice? Do people become singers, actors, filmmakers, writers, or standup comedians so they can finally express themselves?

How can you keep distress from slowly destroying you? Get moving. Even a teenager or a victim of domestic violence can spend a few moments behind the door of the bathroom, even if it's not possible to move out of the living space. If you think you can't get moving, because of some medical problem or other physical limitation, talk to your doctor. He or she wants you to exercise, and you can always do *something*. Physical activity serves a potentially lifesaving need, because the energy release helps balance your nervous system. For some people, physical movement is another form of spiritual practice, with healing and cleansing benefits—that's the very foundation of Yoga, the movements and poses (asanas) are meant to prepare you for meditation. You've heard about endorphins, these are the good guys of the nervous system, released through physical activity.

The beneficial effects of endorphins include less pain, less depression, a stronger immune system, and stress relief. We all need a physical outlet, or stress can literally eat you alive.

It's not selfish to take your "me time" and use it well. If you need to negotiate for that time, do it. You're not being selfish to claim the time to take care of yourself. You are more than entitled to do what keeps you healthy. In fact, if you're a mom, dad or someone's partner, it's selfish when you *don't* do it. If you're not in good shape, you won't be available to act as a parent or partner, and potentially you could become a burden to your loved ones if you developed a chronic illness. Think of the common example of putting on your own oxygen mask on a plane before helping anyone else. Flight attendants always give that instruction, because you're no good to anyone else if you keel over. It's the same thing, if you allow stress to build up and make you sick. You've heard the expression, "Sitting is the new smoking?" It absolutely is. You need to move your body! Help yourself be well. You deserve it.

Since we're family by now, let's talk colonoscopy. My doctor sent me for my first when I turned 50. I wasn't looking forward to it—many people I knew who'd gone through one complained that the prep day was unpleasant: fast all day, then drink a fluid to liquefy and flush out anything remaining in your gut. I was a good patient, I followed instructions, and I have two doses of good news: not just that I passed, but I can tell you it's no big deal. That is, *if you don't eat a toxic diet.*

It's ironic that the abbreviation for the Standard American Diet is SAD. Many of us eat too much processed food, too much bleached white flour, too much sugar, too much meat, and too much saturated fat. The people who suffer through the prep day before their colonoscopies might be miserable because their bodies are so full of toxins. Flushing out all their toxicity can turn a necessary procedure into an uncomfortable chore. Follow me through the metaphor—emptying yourself of emotional toxins accumulated in childhood can be just as challenging and unpleasant.

Here's another metaphor by comparison. Some medicines, like aspirin, can yield quick relief. Others, like antibiotics need to build up in the body over time. Understand what relief it's fair to expect. If you don't feel the effects right away, it doesn't mean it isn't working. The toxicity of a childhood spent in a dysfunctional family works just like the Standard American Diet—the effects accumulate slowly, and it can take some time to lose those effects. Part of your cure may require patience.

You can't remedy a painful upbringing with good nutrition, but you can speed up that recovery by attacking on two fronts. Overcoming a self-esteem-shattering childhood and thriving requires being as deliberate about what you put into your body as about what you put into your self-talk. Fundamental change comes from the inside out, but can also be assisted from the outside in. How you see yourself and talk to yourself reflect your spirituality; think of that as your inner healthful posture. The energy you put out and attract to you, visualizing and meditating in your "me time," serving your fellow human beings, and enjoying your own company and the company of others— those involve some externals. Eating and drinking crap invites toxins into your body, much like beating yourself up invites toxicity into the mind.

For much of my adult life, I assumed that I could drink sodas, eat desserts or big plates of pasta and get away with it, because I worked out hard every day. I found out I was mistaken. I discovered that what you look like on the outside is not a reliable indicator of what's going on inside.

I went for a routine physical when I was in my mid 40s. The usual blood draw showed cholesterol levels, kidney function, etc., were all within normal limits—except for one surprise. My fasting blood sugar was too high. The doctor sent me back for another blood draw, for a hemoglobin A1c test; that measures the average of your blood sugar levels over the previous three months. That was also too high. Looking at the report instead of at me, the doctor said, "That's pre-diabetic." Incredulous, I looked at him and asked, "So what now? You're going to have me on Metformin in a couple years?" He said, "Probably." Now wait a second. I was not overweight, I exercised like a maniac and thought I ate a decent diet. I asked how in the world could I be heading towards diabetes? He shook his head and said, "Well, if it's in your genes…" as if it were already a done deal that I was powerless to change. I walked out of his office stunned and rebellious. I studied nutrition on my own for the next two years. I read textbooks and research articles, watched documentaries, attended lectures and workshops, consulted with dietitians, diabetes educators, and naturopaths. I worked to transcend conventional wisdom, to learn all I could about what good nutrition really is. Since then, I've been mostly vegan, eating a whole-food plant-based diet. I put many raw foods and greens on my plate, without animal products except for a little fish sometimes or occasionally some cheese, staying away from sugar and fast food. The result? My primary care doctor told me he was envious of my most recent set of labs: cholesterol levels, fantastic; A1c test down from 5.9 to 5.3—a big drop in average blood sugar. And let me brag—I have abs again, not bad for a guy in his mid 50s.

Being mindful of what we put into our mouths matters as much to us as the words we send out of our mouths matter to others. Everyone can benefit from better nutrition. It's an observable start for anyone wanting to upgrade his or her life. But what to do? The internet, magazines and TV make dieting and healthy eating advice overwhelming, and often contradictory. It feels like books and infomercials pitching programs, supplements and gizmos come at us non-stop. Fortunately, the basics are easy: bright colored veggies, nuts, seeds, legumes, fruits in moderation. Include healthy fats like avocados, olive oil or salmon; if your paycheck will allow, add sea vegetables, and superfoods like cacao beans, spirulina, and goji berries.

Give yourself permission to experiment—eating well doesn't have to cost an arm and a leg. Specialty markets and health food stores can provide what you need if you shop deliberately. (You may have heard the joke about the store dubbed Whole Paycheck.) It doesn't have to be that way. Plan your meals, and then plan your shopping trip. The experts advise us to "shop the periphery" at the market—better health begins in the Produce and Bulk Foods sections. If you'd like some direction, consider this:

Instead of bacon and eggs, or a bagel with cream cheese for breakfast, what about a bowl of steel cut oatmeal followed by a small palmful of walnuts. (They're much less expensive purchased in the bulk foods section.) The complex carbs and healthy fat burn slower and don't spike your blood sugar. Lunch? Green smoothies made in a blender have become popular, and good-tasting incredibly nutritious recipes are everywhere. (If you have the budget to buy locally grown organic produce, do it!) And, for many people, drinking fruits and vegetables in smoothie form means easier digestion and absorption of the nutrients.

The benefits of great nutrition can be noticeable in even a few days. You may sleep better, have more energy and stamina, and you may feel younger and stronger than your age. Upgrading your nutrition will support everything else you want to accomplish. You can do this, and you don't necessarily have to follow a program. Once you learn to listen to your body's feedback, it will tell you what's good for you. Your only stopper may be wondering if you deserve it. Remember, you'll find that you are exceptional, an example others will want to follow. How much motivation will you get from others' sincere envy? The typical Western diet can be an invitation to trouble. Please include great nutrition as part of loving yourself.

Your relationship with food could be uncomfortable, for many reasons. A lot of painful scenes began at the dinner table, sometimes ignited by dislike of what was put in front of you. Family meals often forced everyone into uncomfortable proximity, making it easier to snipe at each other. Some people use food as a rebellion or as an escape—nurturing themselves with peanut butter cups rather than salad. Now, enjoying a peaceful nutritious meal could feel very unaccustomed.

A landmark study was published in 1998 by Dr. Vincent Felitti from Kaiser Permanente San Diego. The *Adverse Childhood Experiences Study* identified a lot of the mental and physical health risks people face after growing up with trauma and dysfunction. (If you look it up, you will see it is jaw-dropping, mind-blowing, tear-jerking, blood-boiling, and validating—all at the same time.) Researchers found real mental and physical risks stemming from growing up with trauma and dysfunction, including depression, obesity, suicide, substance abuse, and risky sexual behavior leading to STDs. As we grow in self-awareness, we gain the power to change our health destiny—physically and psychologically, and that's encouraging news. The faster you can change it is encouraging, because one of the more disturbing conclusions researchers drew was that the frequency and severity of the effects could be even worse than they reported.

Drug companies and many medical professionals would be out of business if everyone were chronically well. There is no cure for 'dysfunctional' because it's not a disease. Many modern medical problems require long-term prescription drugs, because the problem is managed but not cured. In his wonderful book, *Radical Healing*, Dr. Rudolph Ballantine reminds us that "Skilled and sensitive healers can make a huge difference, but in the final analysis they are only assistants." Modern medicine works to relieve most unpleasant symptoms, while the underlying disease continues, and often progresses. And with the side effects of many medications, sometimes the trade isn't worth it. Your daily diet matters more than you may realize. (For up-to-date, easy to follow information I highly recommend Dr. William Li's book *Eat to Beat Disease*.) The better nourished you are, the better you can feel. Often, your body heals and repairs itself. You are the one responsible for getting and staying well regardless of whatever help you enlist.

Please notice, if you're worried about what you might have to give up for healthy eating, it doesn't have to be about that. Healthful change isn't so much about what you stop doing, but about what you can start doing as a regular daily practice. Eventually, you'll phase out what isn't good for you. Being told

163

to stop doing something inspires resentment and rebellion, whether you're telling it to yourself or hearing it from someone else. Resolving to stop doing something works, but only works for a while. Usually, it's just a matter of time before we fall back into old habits. Remember your New Year's resolutions? Simply stopping an action isn't the answer, we need to *start* doing something else. In nutrition, make it your goal to eat only when you feel hungry; put more vegetables than other foods on your plate; have an apple before going for a pastry; try some raw almonds or cashews before reaching for a sugary dessert; make your sandwiches on sprouted grain bread. When you start making simple additions of wholesome foods, you're making less room for the unhealthy, processed, artery-clogging, sugar and sodium bombs that are so easily grabbable.

Buckminster Fuller has encouraging advice: "The best way to predict the future is to design it." A better future starts within you, with the nutrition you give your body. You have several ways to rebuild your life and your self-esteem, after you leave your childhood household. One demonstrably effective tool is eating a healthy, nutrient-filled diet—and you can start by adding rather than stopping behaviors and feeling punished. Your body will love you for it, and when you look in the mirror you'll be able to at least like what looks back. A self-loving, well-nourished, exceptional person is the one you'll take with you when you go out into the world every day.

Realize that even the way you speak has been transformed by your dysfunctional family—the way you talk to other people, and even more, the way you talk to yourself. Pay attention to the way you use your words; adjusting your life requires adjusting your relationship to yourself. You'll need to replace all that childhood conditioning with training that serves you better. You shape your grammar, syntax, word choices, use of slang, and dialect from your life experience. It all reveals to others how you think, and your idea of yourself. In your speech and actions, what comes out of you is what's inside you.

Using myself as an example, I learned early to be afraid to state opinions confidently; I used to buffer my statements with apologetic words. My lack of self-confidence cropped up in qualifiers: "It's a little cold," "That was kinda rude," "I was fairly happy about it." I even pulled my punches when praising others: rather than "That was delicious," my comment would be "Not bad." Even when I meant the superlative, I phrased it in the diminutive. Especially when talking about a personal success, it was, "I didn't do so bad," or "I did okay." My second-best learned attitude always sneaked out. My childhood conditioning improves daily, but it still requires conscious self-monitoring. [I share this so you can listen to others as well as yourself, and know what they really mean.]

Our behavior and our language spring from the same source feelings. My humor was reflexively self-deprecating. With intention and awareness, it will be easy to change that. Pick one daily action and use it for your private lesson. Decide what job you want your words to do, choose your words deliberately, and make the person you're speaking to feel validated and respected. Use your communication to honor the other person; shift your focus from "How do I sound" to "How will they feel" hearing it? Do this often enough, and people will speak to you more respectfully and kindly, and you will start talking to yourself that way, too. The Persian poet Rumi said, "When you succeed in controlling the words you speak aloud, the words that you speak to yourself may astonish you."

If healthy self-esteem isn't currently your norm, build yourself one. Start with the way you talk. Don't rush, and take time to consider your words. Remember your divine spiritual connection? Send your thoughts there and use what comes up. Your words reflect your inner world—let it reflect respect for yourself and others. Access acceptance of others and yourself. As you learn to make this a habit, it's how you'll also speak to yourself. Go back to your "I Am" affirmations in chapter 6. A good time to try this is as you're walking into work: "I Am part of something special. Everyone gets my best today, and I'll receive theirs." Our old conditioning makes us our own worst critics and judges. Once you intentionally choose the words you speak to others and to yourself—with acceptance, appreciation and respect instead of criticism—you may not realize the immediate benefits, but may feel them, even down to your body's cellular level. Most of the people in your life deserve those benefits, and more importantly, so do you. Keep in mind Viktor Frankl's concept that "Between stimulus and response is choice." Also, the business-world notion that "Problems are opportunities" can re-center you. Choosing your words, tone and facial expression well can turn an adversary into a problem-solving partner.

When you have something angry or ugly to say, don't say it—write it down. The old-fashioned way is to keep a written journal, or you can record your thoughts into your cell phone in private. Say how were affected by your interactions, and what you've learned. For some people, speaking is easier than writing things down; either way, journaling is very therapeutic. Once you can hear or see your thoughts, you can evaluate them. Since you're the only one who will see this, don't worry about "getting it right." (As the cliché says, don't let the Perfect be the enemy of the Good.) Remember, privacy is key: being overheard or leaving your writing around for others to discover could make the situation worse rather than better. You don't have to worry about what anyone else thinks; this is for you to help yourself. So, say what you think and feel, this is just thinking things through for you. You could start to see that you can forgive yourself for mistakes. You may see that you deserve better than you have allowed yourself.

If you're not sure how to begin, start with "The best thing that happened to me today was…" and keep going. What made it the best thing of your day? How did you make it happen, or did it happen to you? Did anyone else play a role? How did you respond? How can you create more of it? Once you've explored that fully, then you can go to the opposite. "The worst thing that happened to me today was…" What made it bad? Could you have handled it differently? What can you do better tomorrow? Remember, you're a work in progress. Do this every day, so your mind is clear for a fresh start tomorrow.

Several years ago, I had a minor fender bender in a parking structure. The guy in front of me in a long line of waiting cars suddenly put his car in reverse and backed into me. We both moved over as much as we could, to let people go around us as we worked things out, but there was nowhere for us to go, and it was a no-win situation. Most of the people behind us saw us and were cool about it, but a 20-something woman screamed and cursed at us as she went by, as though he had hit me just to inconvenience her. I couldn't get over her four-letter tirade for hours. It felt personal, and I was pissed! She was mildly inconvenienced for barely a minute; there was no need for her to be so hateful. How could she be such an ass? I wouldn't have been that mean if the roles had been reversed. Her feelings were the most important thing to her, and she chose to act on them. Even though I knew her hate wasn't really about me, I let my feelings about it spoil my evening. It was a good exercise to talk it out into my cell phone later that night. It took a while, but I dissipated my hurt by realizing that this was the pattern I often experienced as a child, and in my later relationships—receiving someone else's wrath when the incident wasn't even my fault. Knowing myself better now, in any similar situation in the future I know to make the choice to assign any blame where it belongs. What came out of her likely reflects how she was conditioned in her childhood.

"Sticks and stones may break my bones, but words will never hurt me." What a crock! We know how powerful words can be, and the damage they can cause—damage that lasts a lot longer than a break or a bruise. Our childhoods exposed us to all sorts of injuring lines, cutting into us, our siblings, or between our parents. We may not have registered those remarks as criticism or harmful when we were young kids or teenagers, if we'd gotten so used to hearing them that we just accepted them as our "normal" at the time. But hurtful words are like waves crashing into cliffs; their damage accumulates over years and erodes what they hit. Whether the water is trying to harm the cliffs or not, the cliff is still damaged.

The damage by words manifests in lack of self-esteem, lack of self-confidence and poor feelings of self-worth, just to name a few. Other damage can show up as difficulties in relating to other people. The way you talk to yourself is shaped by what you are told.

My mother repeated all through my childhood and into my mid 20s, that I'm ugly. I was adopted as a newborn, and my mom told the story countless times for years and years: she'd tell people that when the nurses brought me out to her, the first words she ever spoke about me were, "Oh my God, that's the ugliest baby I've ever seen." Then she recovered with, "But I love him." She told people that story so many times that it was like a recorded loop as I grew up. To her, it was an amusing anecdote to share with other parents. Looking back now, I can see she was praising herself for accepting this child. I have no way of knowing how many newborns she'd seen fresh out of the womb, but she got a lot of mileage out of that story over the years. It never occurred to her how it made *me* feel to hear it told so often. But her message to me was clear: Ugly...ugly... ugly.

Mom, I was listening, and I've never seen a handsome man looking back at me in the mirror. Of course, what you believe is what you radiate. During my radio career, I was doing a high-profile shift, and the station was planning a billboard campaign for an important ratings period. The campaign planned to put the air staff's pictures up on billboards around town. The program director told me, verbatim, "You're not cosmetically appealing." My picture did not go up. I just said okay. My thoughts and words projected a "face made for radio."

That was decades ago, and today I know I'm a quality individual who has a lot to offer. Even if your upbringing didn't teach you to believe it, so are you! Words have power over us, whether they're delivered with hurtful intention or uplifting intention. Knowing this gives us power; your power comes from how you use your words. Your speech—to yourself, your co-workers, your friends, or your children—shapes more than your relationships, it shapes how others respond to you. Others hear you on more levels than you realize.

Choosing your words carefully also delivers results on many different levels. If you indulge your anger and blurt something you might not mean later, you can hurt someone's feelings. Back-pedaling or apologizing later will not heal the injury. In dysfunctional relationships, those apologies don't often happen, and if they do, they don't erase the damage done by the screaming, put-downs, scary altercations, or physical venting. The hurtful rancor gets absorbed. For children, the absorption can be deep when they're not even aware that it's happening—that's just how daily life is. Personalities develop around it. Toddlers, grade-school children and teenagers don't have the information or resources to say, "Stop! All this venting and venom are overwhelming me, and this trauma will have a very destructive impact on my adult life."

We can't change our past, but we can absolutely change our present, and certainly our tomorrow. A good start for that change is our self-talk, and then the words that spring from it. Redirecting our self-talk includes time for reflection, meditation, repeating affirmations, connecting with our true spiritual identity—and expecting the benefits from them. No technique, exercise or process is going to be of much use if you don't have the confidence that it will. We see this play out in the voice therapy process. Often, patients think that because they already know how to talk they don't need to be taught how to do it. They often DO need to be taught how to do it properly; I have to explain to them that we're not working to change their voice, we're working to tweak the biomechanics. I reassure them that they'll still sound like themselves, hopefully just clearer with less effort, with more vocal stamina and more self-awareness. But therapy won't help them much if they don't think it will. They need to buy into it at least a little and believe it can be beneficial. You're smart, you understand why I'm comparing a process my patients can see to a process you need to visualize. Employing what you're learning will let you improve your experience, and stop being another "adult child from a dysfunctional family."

Now you have the tools to shape your self-talk, and your relationships with everyone, of any age, around you. Now that you know the secrets, it's not complicated. Angry and mean words will hurt and repel whoever you're talking to (including yourself.) Uplifting, affectionate and positive humorous words attract others. Swami Satchidananda, in his book *The Yoga Sutras of Patanjali*, teaches, "You can make or break, bless or

171

curse, with your words." That's just as true about the words you speak to yourself, so watch *all* your words. Speak well.

What if you had to live your life over again? Philosophy professors call this "eternal recurrence," and pose this question in the classroom: What if you had to live your life over and over, the same way, indefinitely? The real underlying question is, would the life you're living now be the one you'd want to repeat? The question is intended to make us stop and think—no, not about Bill Murray or *Groundhog Day*. The point is, to look at our lives, expand our awareness, and consider any changes we should make.

Everyone has daily routines and patterns, and it's human to get stuck in unfulfilling ruts. The danger comes when we become so accustomed to a rut that we think what's "true right now" is supposed to be "true forever." People who come for professional help for chronic laryngitis often need to be reminded that they have become so used to damaging habits that they have begun to think of them as their new "normal." Whether seeking out professional vocal help to correct faulty voicing, or breathing or posture habits, or the damaging attitudes and behaviors from childhood, you deserve to find your way back to what is **natural** for you. The "normal" you're carrying now could reflect your childhood training, but not your adult needs now. The good news is, since you have free will, given to you by your Source, you are self-determining. You can change your patterns.

Your life experiences, your genetics, your education, your social circles and more—they have combined to create your unique personality, and the quality of your life. Your question today should be, who would you like to become? Do you want to be the finest, most loving and lovable person you could be? Spiritually aware and at peace with yourself? How about someone who invites people in, instead of slumping and looking at the ground? How about someone who doesn't fish for others' approval, looking foolish or irritating people in the process? You can make consistent subtle adjustments, one at a time, to make life-changing impacts.

If I may quote Tina Turner, "What's love got to do with it?" We all learned from our parents what love is "supposed" to look like. We develop our ideas of love from the examples, and when you grow up in conflict, distress or anxiety the examples can be twisted. If Tina will excuse me, each individual has his or her own way of expressing and receiving love. How were you shown love as a child? How did your parents show love to each other? Some experiences of love are so idiosyncratic that they're weird. My parents told me they loved me, and they probably meant it when they said it. But between those "I love you" moments would come demoralizing episodes of condemnation, neglect, humiliation, even violence—people indulging their own feelings at the expense of those around them. Watching adults destructively "love" each other, or you, sets the stage for your later heartache and pain.

If your childhood experiences of love involved wild emotional rollercoaster rides, expect that your ideas of giving love and getting love are distorted. And if that's what you've learned about love, what would you expect to attract in your relationships? If you're honest with yourself, do you even know *how* to form the loving, mutual relationships you imagine you see on TV or in movies? In order not to repeat the relationship mistakes we've experienced so far, we need to learn to love in healthier ways.

Smart you, you have this book. Start with the self-respect, self-love and love for others you gain from the ideas in this book. You don't need to be in a romantic relationship to practice loving. With best friends, honored teachers, peers and partners, your daily life is your laboratory for loving in the broader sense. What you can create starts inside of you, with accepting, not with *wanting*. This new behavior might feel risky if you've behaved in a certain way for a long time. Luckily, human potential researchers Herbert Otto and John Mann saw you coming: "Personal growth... takes place when a person has risked himself and dared to become involved in experimenting with his own life." If you've been waiting for permission to dare, now you have it. The rewards are more than worth the initial awkwardness of change, and the reward of becoming the "real you." There's a lot more to Love than just having a Lover. Don't discount universal and spiritual love, which includes your loving YOU. Having a healthy self-love and a loving nature gives off the vibe that can attract affection, and a romantic partner, without effort. You can attract the best-for-you people and circumstances, when your ability to love yourself is repaired. This has nothing to do with ego; it's merely to recognize and appreciate who you really are—a creation of God, created with a purpose.

Can you possibly see yourself as two individuals at the same time? Your family saw you however they did, but you are also a perfect creation, reflecting God-governed intelligent energy. Now that you're out of the environment you grew up in, you are free to be that other exceptional individual. By learning to channel the creative power of your Source, you can realize who are, and who you can be. Take your cue from author Eric Butterworth: "We are human in expression but divine in creation and limitless in potentiality." Love becomes much less confusing when you replace old patterns with new ones, and elevate your consciousness a little.

Getting into sync with the Intelligence-that-created-you doesn't mean you have to "get religious" or knock on doors like a missionary. This seems like the time to say it: if you don't trust yourself yet, would you be willing to invest 3 minutes in trusting me? You and I are on the same team, so let yourself be willing to see yourself as exceptional, and flush the negative influences of your past. It may take some time to feel comfortable with the idea of deserving self-love, but again, that's where you can trust me. You're entitled to whatever time it takes to get used to seeing yourself differently. BTW, the people in your life may also need time to get used to the new, upgraded YOU. Please have as much patience with yourself as you'll have with them, and vice versa. And the sooner you can have that patience, the better.

You never know when an insight will strike, or where, or how. The important thing is, don't dismiss it. In my late 30s, I was in the large butterfly exhibit of a museum one afternoon. Dozens of exotic species of butterflies were displayed and labeled with their details. Looking at the display, I was struck with one of those moments of unexpected connection, the memory of a poem from years ago in a college class—T.S. Eliot's "The Lovesong of J Alfred Prufrock." The people who thought they knew me only knew what I had shown them; and just as these butterflies are frozen in time and pinned to the velvet, some people seeing a change in who they think I am would be as shocked as if one of these pinned specimens flew away. The longer I looked into the boxes, the more depressed I felt. At that time, I felt like those butterflies: "Just give me a label and pin me to the wall." I felt that I was only what others thought I was, narrowly defined and often negatively. We train people how to see us, and I'd accepted other people's definition of me. After I had completed my freshman year of college with a 4.0 grade point average, my friend Rhonda said, "I didn't think you were that smart." She knew me only casually, and was apparently surprised to see my academic accomplishment. That awkward moment only became useful years later, because it showed me what kinds of opinions about me I had allowed. It also showed me what I wanted to change. The realization directed me to start busting out of my pessimistic, self-minimizing rut.

Before that revelation, I'd tried to make changes, but they

were only superficial: my wardrobe, the places where I hung out, changing jobs and cities, even careers. I'm sharing my insights hoping to save you some frustrating effort. I took the path of studying the teachings of great thinkers, spiritual and healing traditions and alternative mind-body disciplines. You can choose your own path—we have all around us truckloads of profound wisdom worth studying, and the thoughts and experiences of spiritually developed thinkers and healers. You already have an introduction to many of those teachings within this book, so you won't have to spend hours at a coffee shop next to a pile of books and a brainload of espresso. (If you choose to do that, you won't be sorry, and you probably know that your best education comes after formal schooling. But you may want to switch to decaf.)

Once we're in the rhythm of adult life, we often don't take enough time to read or study. Much of what occupies our minds is work-related, or fluff and entertainment to escape from daily routine. Some of us are so busy managing obligations, work and family that we don't take time to "study" once we're out of school. (We only have midterms or finals at tax time.) Because of our childhood training, grown-up experiences with other adults can range from confusing to painful to practically intolerable. Since we're often challenged to do better, we need to move beyond the scars from our childhoods. Even if it's not your habit, don't disregard reading. Historian Will Durant says, "It is an error to suppose that books have no influence. It is a slow influence, like flowing water carving out a canyon, but it tells more and more with every year; and no one can pass an hour a day in the society of sages and heroes without being lifted up a notch or two by the company he has kept." If you are inspired to make upgrades, there's a reference list at the end of this book. The thinkers, healers and spiritual leaders throughout history have left us great inspiration in their reflections and insights. You can facilitate your connection to your Divine Source, the Great Intelligence. When you tap into that power, you will be able to manifest a life of more joy and peace and abundance. You don't have to see it with your eyes to benefit from its effects. "You can't see your own diaphragm," as I say to my patients, "but you breathe 24/7. You know it's there and you know it's working, and with intention you can make it work better."

Once you have the insight and are willing to do the work, you can create a positive, self-affirming life and do it on your own terms. If you choose, you are free to start Right Now, and experience the kind of life that you would *enjoy* repeating. That's not a license to live like there's no tomorrow. That's not permission to be reckless. That's the reminder to live a life you appreciate.

Remember the TV show "Quantum Leap?" The science term quantum leap refers to an electron instantly jumping from one orbit of an atom into another orbit of the same atom. People can also have "quantum leap" moments—flashes of game-changing realization. Sometimes quantum leap moments show up during a personal crisis, or during meditation, or whenever. Most of the time, our life journeys take more time and effort – pushing us through lived experiences. Zen Master Okada Torajiro teaches, "I have met all my misfortunes as though they were my honored teachers." Reframing our problems as opportunities to learn makes us accumulate knowledge and wisdom, if we're paying attention.

To go back to the question, what if you had to live your life over again, what would you do differently? You should now have more tools than when you started this book, so you're better prepared to make adjustments. You can become your own repairman or redecorator, and create a life you'll be happy to repeat. The late Dr. Wayne Dyer reminds us that "the wake doesn't drive the boat." He compares our pasts to the wake of a ship—it's the stuff we leave behind as we proceed. The wake is the trail that the ship is constantly moving away from. The ship is under its own power, not the power of the wake behind it.

To take this metaphor one step further, the engine provides the energy for the boat. The "engine" installed during a dysfunctional childhood got you this far, but you'll want to steer it differently to end up at the desired destination. You can even stop looking at your choppy wake, except to notice how much progress you've made to get to this point. Now it's time to enjoy the ride and anticipate where it's taking you. Now you have tools to adjust your course, with your new understanding of your engine.

Remember, YOU are not dysfunctional. Your childhood environment was. YOU are a perfect, Divinely-created 'God particle.' Your goal now is to show up every day with what you've got, know that you have the power to create, and celebrate—your past and your future. If you had to repeat your life again, you could make changes, but you wouldn't have to regret your past: every struggle, frustration and challenge behind you has contributed to making you who you are. That's wonderful, and an adventure, so you can be grateful.

Every morning brings a fresh set of possibilities, and more chances to create what you want. Your life right now is yours— to honor and celebrate or to complain about and lament. You deserve the former. Choose it. You can grow, evolve, discover, and become everything you were created to be. It doesn't matter whether you're a teenager or a senior citizen. Somatic educator Thomas Hanna teaches "Age is nothing more than the accumulation of experience." Let me share the gentleman who put a face on this teaching for me. In my speech pathologist capacity, I saw an elderly gentleman in the hospital who was recovering from a mild stroke. He had a weakened voice and slightly slurred speech. He explained that he owned his own business, and while being driven to work he started slurring his words. Surprised, I said to him, "You *still* go to work every day?" "Of course!" he said. "I'm only 88." He loved what he did and did what he loved. Age was irrelevant.

Yoga classes end with everyone's hands at their Heart Centers and an exchange of "Namaste." From Sanskrit it translates "The light within me honors the light within you," or "The Divine in me bows to the Divine in you." There is Divine in you! Celebrate it, in your life and the lives around you. You come from that Light, and all the qualities of that Creative Intelligent Source are in you. Growing up in a dysfunctional family upsets that for a time, and you may have suffered with lingering results for years after. But you're driving your boat now, with the awareness to connect with your source energy. You can create a life that you would be happy to repeat, one that's downright admirable. You can look back at the wake behind you that your life so far created, and to everyone who has contributed to your journey, and say "Namaste." Look in the mirror, realize who you are, acknowledge the amazing things you've done with what you have, and what you have yet to create. Say "Namaste." You are exceptional.

Life begins Right Now, and today is day one.

And I say to you, Namaste.

CODA

One of my teachers in high school was a Vietnam veteran, and when the movie *Apocalypse Now* came out, he saw it with some of his military buddies. He told us students that as they watched the movie, they would often nod their heads and quietly say "Yeah"—the reality of being a soldier in that war was so well depicted. In this book, I may have elicited some "Yeah" responses, too, from those who know what it's like to grow up in a dysfunctional family, then face the later difficulties and struggles and feel the frustrations. Hopefully, this book has shown you some ways to have a better experience, by redirecting your thoughts, energy and intentions.

Thank you for accompanying me on this journey. If you have gained something helpful and meaningful by reading this, or if you think anything is missing, please feel free to communicate it to me. The journey doesn't end here.

Send your thoughts and comments to:

otherthannormal@yahoo.com

ABOUT THE AUTHOR

Dan Sherwood is a clinical vocologist at the Johns Hopkins Voice Center. His more than 20 years of treating and curing patients' voice, body and breathing problems come after 13 years on-air on radio – he combines his helping profession with personal experience in knowing what vocal athletes need.

He brings even more varied personal experience to his patients: he's overcome the decades of damage incurred growing up in a dysfunctional family. He combines the knowledge and understanding gained from his master's degree in speech pathology from Marquette University and studying voice at the Wisconsin Conservatory of Music, with vocology certification from the National Center for Voice and Speech. He is also a certified Hanna Somatic Educator and Optimal Breathing® coach, and combines his clinical training with mind-body disciplines into a holistic approach to vocal therapy, and in conquering the effects of a dysfunctional family history.

Mr. Sherwood presents at national and international conferences on how to incorporate mind-body practices into traditional vocal rehabilitation, to patients' greatest benefit.

FURTHER READING

A Course in Miracles. Foundation for Inner Peace.

Alexander, Gerda. *Eutony*. Felix Morrow.

Anderson, Uell S. (2017). *Three Magic Words*. Stellar Classics.

Ballentine, Rudolph. (1999). *Radical Healing*. Three Rivers Press.

Barks, Coleman & Moyne, John (Trans.). (1999). *The Essential Rumi*. Penguin Books.

Benner, Joseph. (2015). *The Impersonal Life*. Merchant Books.

Borysenko, J. (1987). *Minding the Body, Mending the Mind*. Bantam Books.

Briggs, John & Peat, F. David. (1999). *Seven Life Lessons of Chaos*. Harper Perennial.

Butterworth, Eric. (1982). *In the Flow of Life*. Unity Books.

Cain, Susan. (2012). *Quiet*. Broadway Books.

Chidvilasananda, Swami. (1996). *The Yoga of Discipline*. Syda Foundation.

Church, Dawson (Ed.). (2004). *The Heart of Healing*. Elite Books.

Church, Dawson. (2014). *The Genie in Your Genes*. Energy Psychology Press.

Csikszentmihaly, Mihaly. (1997). *Finding Flow*. Basic Books.

Damasio, A. (2010). *Self Comes to Mind.* Pantheon Books.

Dispenza, Joseph. (2012). *Breaking the Habit of Being Yourself.* Hay House, Inc.

Dürckheim, Karlfried Graf. (2004). *Hara.* Inner Traditions.

Dyer, Wayne. (1998). *Wisdom of the Ages.* William Morrow.

Emoto, Masaru. (2001). *The Hidden Messages in Water.* Atria Books.

Fahey, B. (1989). *The Power of Balance.* Metamorphous Press.

Feldenkrais, Moshe. (1985). *The Potent Self.* Frog, Ltd.

Ferrucci, P. (2004). *What We May Be.* Jeremy P. Tarcher.

Ford, Debbie. (1998). *The Dark Side of the Light Chasers.* Riverhead Books.

Forward, S & Buck, C. (1989). *Toxic Parents.* Bantam Books.

Galwey, T. (2000). *The Inner Game of Work.* Random House.

Gleick, James. (1987). *Chaos.* Penguin Books.

Goldsmith, Joel. (1963). *A Parenthesis in Eternity.* Harper San Francisco.

Golomb, E. (1992). *Trapped in the Mirror.* Quill.

Goswami, Amit. (1993). *The Self-Aware Universe.* Jeremy P. Tarcher.

Grossinger, Richard. (1995). *Planet Medicine.* North Atlantic

Books.

Hanna, Thomas. (Ed.). (1978). *Explorers of humankind.* Harper & Row.

Hanna, Thomas. (1979). *The Body of Life.* Alfred A. Knopf.

Hartley Linda. (1995). *Wisdom of the body moving.* North Atlantic Books.

Hawkins, David. (1995). *Power vs. Force.* Hay House, Inc.

Heller, Joseph & Henkin, William. (1986). *Bodywise.* North Atlantic Books.

Holmes, Earnest. (1950). *How to Use the Science of Mind.* Science of Mind Publishing.

Hunt, Valerie. (1989). *Infinite Mind.* Malibu Publishing Co.

Johari, Harish. (1989). *Breath, Mind, and Consciousness.* Destiny Books.

Johnson, Don Hanlon (Ed.). (1995). *Bone, Breath & Gesture: Practices of Embodiment.* North Atlantic Books.

Juhan, Deane. (1987). *Job's Body.* Station Hill Press.

Klein, Jean. (1994). *Beyond Knowledge.* Non-Duality Press.

Knaster, Mirka. (1996). *Discovering the Body's Wisdom.* Bantam Books.

Kohl, Herbert. (1994). *I Won't Learn from You: and Other Thoughts on Creative Maladjustment.* W.W. Norton & Co.

Krishnamurti, J. (1973). *The Awakening of Intelligence.* Harper One.

Levine, Peter. (1997). *Waking the Tiger.* North Atlantic Books.

Li, William. (2019). *Eat to Beat Disease.* Vermilion.

Lipton, Bruce. (2008). *The Biology of Belief.* Hay House, Inc.

Littlewood, William & Roche, Mary Alice (Eds.). (2004). *Waking Up.* Author House.

Maitland, Jeffrey. (1994). *Spacious Body.* North Atlantic Books.

Martin, Paul. (1998). *The Healing Mind.* St. Martin's Press.

McTaggert, Lynne. (2007). *The Intention Experiment.* Free Press.

Mitchell, Stephen. (1988). *Tao Te Ching.* Harper Perennial.

Myss, Caroline. (1996). *Anatomy of the Spirit.* Harmony Books.

Ober, Clinton; Sinatra, Stephen & Zucker, Martin. (2010). *Earthing.* Basic Health Publications, Inc.

Otto, Herbert & Mann, John. (1968). *Ways of Growth.* Grossman Publishers.

Pallaro, Patrizia. (Ed.). (2007). *Authentic Movement.* Jessica Kingsley Publishers.

Pearsall, Paul. (2003). *The Beethoven Factor.* Hampton Roads Publishing.

Pert, Candace. (1997). *Molecules of Emotion*. Scribner.

Prem, Sri Krishna. (2008). *The Yoga of the Bhagavad Gita*. Morning Light Press.

Ratley, John & Hagerman, Eric. (2008). *Spark*. Quercus.

Roberts, Jane. (1972). *Seth Speaks*. Prentice-Hall.

Sacks, Rabbi Jonathan. (2011). *The Great Partnership*. Schoken Books.

Sarno, John. (2007). *The Divided Mind*. Harper Collins.

Satchidananda, Sri Swami. (1978). *The Yoga Sutras of Patanjali*. Integral Yoga Publications.

Satchidananda, Sri Swami. (1988). *The Living Gita*. Integral Yoga Publications.

Scaer, Robert. (2001). *The Body Bears the Burden*. The Haworth Medical Press.

Shanklin, Imelda. (1929). *What are You?* Unity House.

Siegel, Daniel J. (2010). *Mindsight*. Bantam Books.

Spaulding, Baird T. (1924). *Life and Teaching of the Masters of the Far East*. Devorrs & Co.

Strozzi Heckler, Richard. (1984). *The Anatomy of Change*. North Atlantic Books.

Strozzi Heckler, Richard (Ed.). (1985). *Aikido of the New Warrior*. North Atlantic Books.

Teilhard De Chardin, Pierre. (1964). *The Future of Man.* Harper Collins.

Templeton, John Marks. (1997). *Worldwide Laws of Life.* Templeton Press.

The I AM Discourses. (1935). Saint Germain Press, Inc.

Tiller, W.A., Dibble, W.E., & Kohane, M.J. (2001). *Conscious acts of creation: The emergence of a new physics.* Pavior Publishing.

Twerski, Abraham. (1992). *Living Each Day.* Mesorah Publications, Ltd.

Twyman, James. (2008). *The Moses Code.* Hay House, Inc.

Walker, Brian. (1992). *Hua Hu Ching: The Unknown Teachings of Lao Tzu.* Harper San Francisco.

Waldrop, M. Mitchell. (1992). *Complexity.* Simon & Schuster.

Walsch, Neale Donald. (1995). *Conversations with God.* Hodder & Stoughton.

Zukav, Gary. (1979). *The Dancing Wu Li Masters.* William Morrow.